PRIVATE-OWNER WAGONS
in Colour
For the Modeller and Historian

David Ratcliffe

Ian Allan
PUBLISHING

First published 2009

ISBN 978 0 7110 3365 8

© David Ratcliffe 2009

Published by Ian Allan Publishing

an imprint of Ian Allan Publishing Ltd, Hersham, Surrey, KT12 4RG
Printed in England by Ian Allan Printing Ltd, Hersham, Surrey, KT12 4RG

Code: 0904/B2

Visit the Ian Allan Publishing website at www.ianallanpublishing.com

Previous page: Following its purchase of ICI's quarrying interests Buxton Lime Industries obtained a Section 8 grant towards a fleet of twenty 67.5-tonne-capacity air-braked hoppers. Although to a Powell Duffryn design they were built abroad by Tatrastroj Poprad of Slovakia, a trend that would continue in future years. BLI 19200-19 took over the Tunstead–Hindlow traffic in 1995. They have also been used to carry limestone to the flue-gas desulphurisation plant at Ratcliffe-on-Soar Power Station and to a Tarmac stone terminal at Pendleton, in west Manchester. The Hindlow trains must reverse at Buxton and BLI 19212, coded JGA, was seen in the overgrown Up Reversing Sidings on 25 July 1998.

CONTENTS

Left: The 35-ton 15ft-wheelbase vacuum-braked tanks played an important part in the story of the private-owner wagon and numerous examples were built not only by Charles Roberts but also Metro-Cammell and Powell Duffryn. When larger tanks were introduced Esso sold some of its Class B 35-tonners to the Central Electricity Generating Board. Renumbered as CEGB 48500-49 they were then used to carry fuel oil from Lindsey refinery to the power stations at Drakelow, Meaford and Willington. However, by February 1988 many were to be found in store at Castle Donington including CEGB 48548, a Powell Duffryn-built example, previously ESSO 43931.

INTRODUCTION

In this book I have considered some of the non-ferry registered privately owned (PO) wagons that came to play such an important role on Britain's rail network in the last quarter of the 20th century, with particular reference to the various commodities they carried and the traffic flows that they operated.

The heyday of the private-owner wagon had appeared to be over when, at the beginning of World War 2, the control of all wagons capable of general use passed to the Ministry of War Transport in an attempt to improve utilisation and eliminate the unnecessary movement of empty vehicles. The majority of those taken over were the traditional five- and seven-plank opens used to carry coal and coke, and as hostilities dragged on their colourful liveries gradually weathered and faded. Those that survived the rigours of wartime conditions passed into British Railways ownership at Nationalisation in 1948 to eke out their few remaining years anonymously in common use, renumbered in the 'Pxxxxxx' series.

The PO wagons to escape wartime pooling and subsequent nationalisation included types such as tipplers, which required special unloading facilities, and tanks, built to handle specific commodities, such as oil or acids. However, during the war years there had been few opportunities to repair existing stock, let alone purchase replacements, and so most remaining fleets were composed of elderly vehicles, many built before the 1923 Grouping, and which were rapidly approaching the end of their useful lives. Furthermore, in the early 1950s, as the railway system slowly recovered and BR began developing new and innovative wagon types, the private ownership of all but tank wagons was discouraged.

Fortunately in 1957 came the first of a number of changes which were to lead to the private owners' renaissance when a new, 35-ton-glw (gross laden weight) tank wagon design was developed as a result of collaboration between Esso Petroleum, British Railways and the long-established wagon builder Charles Roberts. Three prototype wagons were built: Class A and Class B tanks, both for Esso, and a creosote tank for BR, all incorporating many of the developments which BR had begun adopting as standard for its own fleet under the 1955 Modernisation Plan. The tanks not only had an increased capacity over earlier types but, more importantly, were fitted with roller-bearing axleboxes and automatic vacuum

brakes, which, combined with their 15ft wheelbase, enabled high-speed operation in block-train formations. The design was an immediate success and quickly went into production not just for Esso but also for several other petroleum and chemical companies.

In 1962 the axle-load limit was raised, first to 20 tons allowing a glw of 40 tons, and, shortly thereafter, to 22½ tons with concomitant minor increases to the loading-gauge. However, the size of tank needed to accommodate such loadings made it necessary to adopt a new 'monobloc' design whereby the chassis cross-members dropped below solebar height, and in place of the anchor or saddle mountings, as used on earlier vehicles, the barrel was secured to the underframe by means of wing plates riveted to the top of the solebar.

This continuous mounting gave extra rigidity and reduced barrel stresses while riveting allowed the tank to be removed from the chassis if necessary. The first monobloc tanks had 10-plate bearing springs, but in 1963 BR decided to introduce the *Union Internationale des Chemins de Fer* (UIC) double-link suspension. At the time this suspension was considered the only one capable of 60mph running at a 22½-ton axle load and accordingly, the growing numbers of 45-ton monobloc tank wagons were so fitted, albeit with 13-plate bearing springs to handle the higher load.

For many years the potential superiority of bogie wagons had been recognised for high-speed operation but it was not until BR raised its permitted axle loading again to 25 tons per axle in 1966 that the higher cost, when compared with a two-axle vehicle, could be justified. Consequently it became possible to design a bogie Class A tank capable of carrying 20,500gal compared with the 17,280gal capacity of two 45-ton

Above: Aggregate companies were amongst the most successful in obtaining grant aid towards new freight facilities and equipment, and also introduced many colourful and attractive liveries to the freight scene. One of the author's favourites was that adopted by Bardon Hill Quarries Ltd as seen in this view of BHQ 17110 taken at Bardon Hill on 17 September 1993. This was one of 21 90-tonne-glw bogie hoppers, BHQ 17101-21, TOPS code PHA, purchased from W. H. Davis in 1986 to replace the ageing fleet of BR 27-ton MSV wagons on the thrice-weekly working to Thorney Mill (West Drayton).

Class A four-wheelers, and it was not long before the oil companies were investing heavily in these new, 100-ton wagons.

The improved economics of rail transport made possible by larger wagons and faster transits were further enhanced by the negotiation of long-term contracts with BR. In return for a highly competitive rate the oil companies agreed to place a minimum level of traffic on rail each year, but this proved to be no burden as demand for petroleum products soared by well over 100% in less than a decade. With hindsight one might question the value of such deals to BR, for while the tonnage of petroleum products carried by rail rose from 4.8 million in 1961 to over 15 million in 1968, revenue per ton was halved. However, when placed within a wider context the development of a nationwide network of about 300 rail-fed oil terminals, supported by more than 400 block trains running every week, changed the perception of railfreight and helped encourage other companies, particularly in the construction industry, to invest in their own wagons.

By the early 1970s British Rail policy had come full circle and from then on it would

Left: While the TOPS system proved to be a godsend to both private wagon owners and BR in improving the operation of the freight network, there were the odd anomalies. When they were first rolled out the decision to differentiate 51-tonne-glw tank wagons had not been made and as a result several fleets were lettered 'TT' before the 'TU' coding was decided upon. Over time as the wagons went through works this was changed but some carried the 'TT' coding all their lives and 51-tonners TRL 70726 and TRL 70717 were recorded at Immingham Reception Sidings in March 1991 still coded TTA. Built by Standard Wagon in 1977 to carry caustic soda from the ICI works at Runcorn they were, by this date, in Atochem caustic soda traffic from Immingham Dock Tank Farm.

only provide wagons for general-merchandise traffic and for the other nationalised industries and government departments. Other customers would now be expected to provide their own vehicles, not only for new traffics, but also to replace life-expired railway-owned wagons used to carry existing flows. Naturally this about turn was not welcomed by everyone and some freight was lost to road, although in many instances these were short-distance workings for which an investment in new rolling stock could not be justified.

A further boost to the PO wagon came with the Transport Act 1974, which provided for direct Government support in the form of Section 8 Grant aid where the use of rail would result in significant benefit to the environment. A maximum grant of 60% of the approved capital cost of new freight facilities and wagons was available and successful applicants could claim Corporation Tax relief on their share of the costs. Grants ranging from as little as £9,000 to over £2 million were awarded, and in the 10 years following its introduction it was estimated that the scheme was responsible for an additional 35 million tonnes of rail-borne freight.

Although many companies purchased their own wagons another option was to lease vehicles from one of the major hire companies such as Algeco (the Belgian subsidiary of German firm VTG), BRTE (British Railway Traffic & Electric, subsequently part of Procor), E. G. Steele & Co Ltd, Railease (a subsidiary of the Standard Wagon Co), STS (Storage & Transport Systems) or Tank Rentals Ltd (a Charles Roberts subsidiary, later spun-off as Tiger Railcar Leasing). Apart from the smaller initial financial outlay involved in

leasing, another advantage was that the hire companies made all the arrangements for the maintenance of their wagons. Indeed, following various takeovers and mergers Procor acquired Charles Roberts, while STS owned Marcroft Engineering, a wagon-repair company with shops at Coalville, Radstock and Burry Port. Furthermore, when the terms of a lease extended beyond that of the vehicle's full 15-year depreciation the rental was reduced to a peppercorn figure, sometimes as low as £1 per wagon per annum.

The interests of the private-wagon industry were represented by the Private Wagon Federation, an umbrella organisation of six autonomous bodies — the Association of Private Railway Wagon Operators, the Association of British Railway Carriage & Wagon Manufacturers, the Wagon Repairing Association, the Wagon Hirers' Association, the Oil Industry Association and the Chemical Industry Association. Members of the Association of British Railway Carriage & Wagon Manufacturers, which included all the established builders, were required to design and manufacture vehicles in compliance with regulations issued by British Rail, while members of the Wagon Repairing Association undertook to carry out maintenance, repair and modification along similar lines. The most important companies involved in the maintenance of private-owner wagons were C. C. Crump & Co at Connah's Quay, Railcar Services Ltd, which had its major works at Horbury, Stoke and Swansea, the aforementioned Marcroft Engineering, Powell Duffryn at Cardiff, and E. G. Steele & Co at Hamilton. The Central Wagon Co at Wigan and South Staffs Wagon at Tipton also undertook a limited amount of repair work, as did W. H. Davis at Shirebrook.

By 1984 there were approximately 15,000 PO wagons in use — roughly 20% of the total freight stock. However, in terms of tonnes per mile they accounted for around 40%. When coal and coke were excluded from the reckoning then two-thirds of all tonne-mileage was in private-owner wagons, and by the end of the decade PO stock accounted for more than 50% of all freight tonnage.

Changes in operating methods also made wagon ownership a more attractive proposition. The introduction of fully fitted block workings resulted in considerably improved utilisation and from the early 1970s company trains for the aggregate and chemical industries had begun appearing in the Working Timetables alongside the established petroleum services. Smaller wagonload flows were not overlooked, for in 1972 the British Railways Board had introduced its 'Air-braked Network' of high-speed, exclusively air-braked, overnight trunk services, which was to be expanded and rebranded as 'Speedlink' in 1977.

In contrast to the old-fashioned wagonload freight system, which had suffered from problems of low speed, frequent remarshalling and unreliable service, the Speedlink network was based on a number of carefully monitored trains linking no more than a dozen or so main yards where they exchanged traffic. There was no marshalling in the traditional sense *en route*, trains stopping only to exchange pre-formed sections, so that a wagon would only be shunted twice, once in its originating area and again at its destination. Such was the success of Speedlink that many customers, including household names like Campbell's Soups, now considered Railfreight as an attractive proposition for small-volume flows. Indeed, some operators found it worthwhile to place a single vehicle on rail.

Another development of considerable benefit to the wagon operator was the adoption by BR of a real-time computer system to regulate its entire operations. Developed from a system pioneered by the Southern Pacific Railroad in the USA, it was gradually introduced in Britain from 1971, spreading to include the entire network by 1975. Known by its acronym TOPS, the Total Operations Processing System recorded each event affecting a vehicle as it happened, allowing for the constant monitoring of an individual wagon's movements and availability.

In order to provide information in a straightforward and uniform manner compatible with the needs of a computerised system of control every freight location was allocated a five-digit numerical identity, while a new set of wagon codes was devised to replace the antiquated telegraphic codes formerly in use. The new TOPS codes were based on a four-letter code in which each letter conveyed information, and which, when taken together, provided a detailed description of the vehicle. The first letter defined the broad wagon type to which the individual vehicle belonged while the second letter defined more exactly the wagon type in question (see Table 1). The third letter indicated the brake type of the wagon, referring to the fitting of through pipes where appropriate, as well as to the provision of full automatic brakes (see Table 2). The fourth letter referred to sub-divisions within each type.

To assist rail staff the first three letters of the TOPS code were included on a wagon's information panel, normally to be found painted on the side of the vehicle. The panel would also carry details as to the tare weight of the wagon, expressed in kilograms, and its capacity as measured in metric tonnes. The bottom line of the panel carried the wagon's unique TOPS number. This consisted of a four- or five-digit number (i.e. a figure between 1000 and 99999), prefixed by an abbreviated form of the owner's name, consisting of up to four letters.

Before the introduction of TOPS each wagon owner had allocated their own numbering policy with the result that some numbers, particularly those below 100, were repeated over and over again. Therefore, all existing wagons had to be renumbered to comply with the new system, which in part accounted for the time taken over its introduction, while all new stock built after 1975 was allocated a previously unused number. A wagon's TOPS number was also

carried on small plastic plates fixed to the solebar.

The opportunity was taken to group together different wagon types within certain number ranges, with most open wagons given numbers below 10,000 while tank wagons of less than 45 tons found themselves numbered between 40xxx and 48xxx and bogie tanks occupied the 7xxxx and 8xxxx ranges. However, over time as certain number blocks became full this was not always possible to sustain. To ensure the integrity of the system each number was unique and until the late 1990s there were no cases of a number being reused, let alone duplicated. Initially, the only alteration to a wagon number would occur in the case of major rebuilding, when a fresh four- or five-digit number would be allocated, or in the case of a change of ownership which would normally be reflected simply by a change of prefix. A number of wagons acquired by both Shell and British Petroleum also saw a change to their TOPS numbers so as to conform to the number coding used by those companies.

Initially, non-ferry PO wagons were coded in the 'P' and 'T' groups, but as new types were introduced it became increasingly difficult to reflect the various differences. This was particularly true with regard to British-registered international ferry wagons, all of which had been lumped under the 'PI' coding. However, by 1991 the withdrawal of BR's vacuum-braked steel carriers had freed up the 'J' and 'K' groups and so a wholesale recoding exercise was undertaken. Since rail privatisation the distinction between formerly railway-owned and PO stock has become somewhat blurred. For example, one batch of bogie tanks introduced by EWS and given six-digit numbers (traditionally allocated to railway-owned stock) were classified 'TEA' (a private-owner coding), while the renumbering of PO stock after a change of ownership has become more commonplace.

Of course, the introduction of TOPS not only made life easier for wagon owners; it was also a great boon to the lucky enthusiast, with access to the system and tracking down the whereabouts of specific fleets became relatively straightforward. Furthermore, TOPS could also provide details of a wagon's lading, originating point and destination and so over time the diligent researcher could build up a comprehensive picture of freight flows throughout the country.

My own serious interest in rail freight began in the spring of 1982 while waiting on Edge Hill station with my fiancée for a delayed multiple-unit to Manchester. As the

time passed we watched as a Class 40 shunted back and forth with a long line of mixed stock including several oddly shaped wagons lettered 'PRESTWIN' and 'TRIPOLY' that had clearly seen better days. Although I had been a rail fan in the broadest sense for as long as I could remember, having grown up with a view of the old LNWR Eccles Junction–Springs Branch line from my bedroom window, and within earshot of Patricroft shed, I was no wagon expert, so when Ruth innocently asked me to explain these markings I was stumped.

The following week, with help from the Head of Chemistry at the college where Ruth and I both taught, I discovered that sodium tripolyphosphate was a constituent of washing powder. Then, later that month, on a visit to the Sherratt & Hughes bookshop in St Anne's Square, Manchester, I chanced upon David Larkin's Bradford Barton volumes *BR Standard Wagons* and *Private Owner Freight Wagons*. Not only did David explain what a Prestwin was, but his books also opened my eyes to the immense variety of rolling stock and to the diverse commodities they carried.

I was hooked, and later that year, when Ruth and I were on holiday in Scotland, I purchased my first decent camera and began to record the freight scene, the beginnings of a collection that at the last count numbered well over 20,000 prints and slides. It was a good time to begin, coinciding as it did not only with the arrival of increasing numbers of private-owner wagons, but also reasonably affordable colour film.

Producing this book — hopefully the first in a short series covering different aspects of the wagon fleet — would not have been possible without the considerable help afforded me by numerous organisations and individuals. In particular, I should like to thank fellow Railfreight Archive members Trevor Mann, David Monk-Steel, Mark Saunders and Hywel Thomas, for permission to include photos from their own extensive collections, and also to acknowledge the contribution of the late Colin Wright, whose enthusiasm kept me going at the end of many a long day's 'wagoning'. I should also like to thank all those railway staff that I have met, the length and breadth of the country, for their kindness in granting me access to their yards and goods depots. Sadly, a road accident many years ago means that Ruth is no longer with me to share in the fruits of my labours, and it is to her memory that this book is dedicated.

David Ratcliffe
Swinton
January 2009

Table 1: Private-owner wagons (TOPS code groups 'J', 'K', 'P' and 'T')

Code	Description	Pre-1991 code
JA	Bogie Covhop	PB
JB	Bogie Covhop	PB
JC	Bogie Presflo	PD
JD	Bogie Bolster D	PX
JE	Bogie hopper	PH
JF	Bogie hopper, aluminium/prototype	PH
JG	Bogie aggregate hopper	PH
JH	Bogie limestone hopper	PH
JI	Bogie Covhop, *RIV*	PI
JJ	Bogie steel	PX
JK	Bogie Lowliner	PF
JL	Bogie two-tier car carrier	PL
JO	Bogie open with cargo winches	PN
JP	Bogie open, pallet	PN
JQ	Bogie side tippler	PT
JR	Bogie open, general/aggregate	PI/PX
JS	Bogie coil	PX
JT	Bogie ironstone tippler outer	PT
JT	Bogie in-line tippler	PT
JU	Bogie ironstone tippler inner	PT
JV	Bogie Carflat	PF
JW	Bogie Palvan	PW
JX	Bogie open, steel scrap	PX
JY	Bogie open	PH
KA	Two-axle special flat	PF
KB	Match/barrier	PX
KC	Escort/weedkilling train coach	PP
KD	Two-axle flask/Trailer-Train	PX
KE	Bogie container flat	PF
KF	Bogie flat/Warflat	PF
KG	Two-axle container flat, *RIV*	PI
KH	Two-axle Presflo, *RIV*	PI
KI	Bogie steel coil, *RIV*	PI
KJ	Self-discharge train transfer vehicle	PX
KK	Two-axle Covhop, *RIV*	PI
KL	Two-axle open high side, *RIV*	PI
KM	Match/barrier/hot core	PX
KN	Dummy flask	PX
KP	Two-axle hopper, *RIV*	PI
KR	Ramp	PX
KT	Mobile tank training vehicle	PX
KV	Large van, *RIV*	PI
KW	Warwell/Weltrol	PF/PX
KX	Bogie flask/Flatrol	PX
KY	Bogie flask, *RIV*	PI
PA	Two-axle Covhop, china clay/dolime/sand	PA
PB	Two-axle Covhop, grain/lime	PA
PC	Two-axle Presflo	PC
PD	Two-axle Cemflo	PC
PE	Two-axle Tip-Air	PE
PF	Two-axle container flat	PF
PG	Two-axle hopper	PG

Code	Description	Pre-1991 code
PH	Self-discharge train hopper	PG
PJ	Cartic	PJ
PK	Three-axle Comtic	PK
PM	Two-axle mineral, no doors	PM
PN	Two-axle open, aggregate/blocks/coal	PO
PO	Two-axle open, steel scrap	PO
PQ	Three-axle Autic	PQ
PR	Two-axle china clay, curtain roof	PR
PS	Two-axle ironstone tippler	PS
PT	Two-axle Palvan	PV
PU	Two-axle van/Palvan	PV
PV	Two-axle Palvan, curtain sides	PV
PX	Two-axle coil/single bolster/tube	PX
TA	Bogie tank, 40-69 tonnes glw	TA
TB	Bogie tank, 70-79 tonnes glw	TB
TC	Bogie tank, 80-89 tonnes glw	TC
TD	Bogie tank, 90-99 tonnes glw	TD
TE	Bogie tank, over 100 tonnes glw	TE
TI	Tank, *RIV*	TI
TM	Three-axle tank, 25 tonnes glw	TM
TR	Two-axle tank, 20-29 tonnes glw	TR
TS	Two-axle tank, 30-39 tonnes glw	TS
TT	Two-axle tank, 40-49 tonnes glw	TT
TU	Two-axle tank, over 50 tonnes glw	TU

Notes:

a) In 1998 the PD and PM codes were reallocated to two-axle van, MoD, and two-axle Palvan, MoD, respectively.

b) *RIV* refers to the *Reglomento Internazionale Vagoni* and covers ferry wagons.

Table 2: TOPS brake type codes
(used as a suffix to the two-letter codes listed in Table 1)

A	Air-braked
B	Air-braked with through vacuum pipe
F	Vacuum-braked with Accelerate Freight Inshot (AFI)
G	Vacuum-braked with AFI and through air pipe
H	Dual air and vacuum-braked with vacuum AFI
O	Unfitted (no automatic brake)
P	Unfitted with through vacuum pipe
Q	Unfitted with through air pipe
R	Unfitted with through air and vacuum pipes
V	Vacuum-braked
W	Vacuum-braked with through air pipe
X	Dual air and vacuum-braked

1. AGGREGATE HOPPERS

Right: The huge motorway building programme of the early 1970s coupled with unprecedented investment in company property, particularly in London and the Thames Valley, saw many quarrying firms turn to rail to provide an economical means of bulk transport.

One such company was Amalgamated Roadstone (subsequently Amey Roadstone Co), which began moving over half a million tonnes of limestone a year from its quarries at Whatley and Tytherington to railheads at Totton, near Southampton, and Wolverton, in Buckinghamshire. To transport the stone it purchased from Charles Roberts 64 new 51-tonne-glw PGA two-axle air-braked hoppers — AR 14201-24 in 1972, and AR 14225-64 in 1973/4. Like many private-owner wagons they were painted in an eye-catching livery, as demonstrated by AR 14218, seen at Tytherington in May 1973. All were fitted with BSC friction-pedestal suspension and could carry an impressive 37.5 tonnes, but unusually for this type, they were built without end platforms.

Above: Such was the success of its rail operation that by the end of the decade ARC had leased an additional 99 PGAs from Procor and opened terminals at Ashford, Ardingly, Maidstone, Theale and West Drayton, while in the 1980s continued traffic growth saw regular workings to Bat & Ball, Hothfield and Tolworth. The ARC fleet was not just confined to southern England for in 1986 a dozen PGAs were used to move agricultural lime from Shap Quarry to farmers in south-west Scotland with unloading points established at both Dumfries and Stranraer. These vehicles generally ran in fully fitted block company train formations of 25 wagons or so, the exact length varying according to the capacity of the different receiving points, but the agricultural lime moved in rafts of five or six wagons at a time via the Speedlink wagonload network, while individual wagons could also be spotted in mixed freights when running to and from repair.

Following the closure of Radstock wagon works in 1988, ARC hoppers occasionally turned up at Railcar Services in Stoke-on-Trent, where AR 14216 was photographed in May of that year. Note that as well as a repaint into mustard and grey the ARC wagons had been fitted with ladders and an end platform along with a deflection plate to protect the brake gear from spilled stone during loading. Presumably built without these features to save weight, the lack of an inspection platform had caused problems when carrying fine stone or dust. When wet such loads had a tendency to compact in transit and when being unloaded might have needed some encouragement with a long stick or shovel to prevent them sticking to the hopper sides.

Above: In 1990 ARC replaced its PGAs with a new fleet of 146 PHA 102-tonne-glw bogie hoppers built by Standard Wagon ('Outers' ARC 17901-32 and 'Inners' ARC 19800-91) and Procor ('Inners' ARC 19892-913). All were fitted with LTF (low track force) bogies and carried 80 tonnes, the 'Inners' having AAR (Association of American Railroads) auto-couplers at both ends while the 'Outers' had conventional buffing gear at one end only. Bringing up the rear of the daily service from Whatley, ARC 17917, now recoded JHA, was about to enter the unloading shed at Theale when seen in September 1991.

Below: The 22 'Inners' built by Procor were easily identifiable by their distinctive body profile, and in 1999, along with the rest of the fleet, began to be repainted in the colours of ARC's parent company, Hanson. ARC 19900 had just been repainted following routine maintenance at Stoke in April 2000. In recent years these wagons have also worked from the ARC quarries at Machen and Penmaenmawr and from RMC's Doveholes Quarry at Peak Forest.

Right: Foster Yeoman had been using rail since the 1920s to supply the local market in Somerset and Wiltshire, but in 1970 it opened a new loading facility at Merehead Quarry and by 1979 was forwarding over three million tons of limestone a year to terminals throughout South East England and the Home Counties. Foster Yeoman also owned a granite quarry at Glensanda on the western shores of Loch Linnhe in Scotland, and from 1989 much of its output was shipped to the Isle of Grain, from where it was sent by rail to the Channel Tunnel construction sites at Shakespeare Cliff and Sevington. Foster Yeoman had also introduced a fleet of 51-tonne-glw PGA hoppers in the early 1970s, eventually totalling nearly 200 wagons, but in contrast to ARC chose to lease rather than purchase outright from the outset. PR 14006, one of the original batch of 25 hoppers, PR 14000-24, built by Charles Roberts at Horbury Junction in 1972, was to be found 20 years later awaiting repair in the cripple sidings at Grain.

Left: In 1989 Foster Yeoman leased 100 new 102-tonne-glw bogie hoppers from the German builder Orenstein & Koppel, numbered OK 19300-99, the first 20 of which were 'Outers'. The new wagons took over the stone traffic from Merehead with regular block workings to the Yeoman terminals at Acton, Botley, Eastleigh, Theale and Wootton Bassett. OK 19371 had recently been repainted when recorded on a rather windy day at Westbury in October 2000. When delivered these wagons had two narrow blue bands at cantrail and solebar height with the Yeoman name in white on a blue rectangular patch.

Right: The boom in aggregate traffic was also felt in the Peak District and in 1977 Tarmac purchased 33 PGAs to carry limestone from Topley Pike Quarry, near Buxton, to terminals in Pendleton, Stockport and Widnes. Following two further orders in 1979, the original Standard Wagon-built batch, TAMC 14655-87, was transferred to Cliffe Hill Quarry in Leicestershire from where they carried granite to the Tarmac terminals at Hayes & Harlington and Hothfield. Hayes also received trainloads of limestone from Frome and Wirksworth and in the 1990s these wagons were also used to bring in gritstone from Cwmbargoed and sand from Marks Tey. Typical of the two-axle aggregate hoppers built in the early 1970s with flat-sided solebars, TAMC 14680 waits to return to traffic having just been overhauled and repainted at Stoke in May 1991. Note that these wagons had the side-stiffening ribs on the outside of the hopper body.

Left: Tarmac's second batch of PGAs, TAMC 14840-70, were built by Procor in 1979 and, in common with others from that date, were to a modified design featuring a steeper slope to the hopper sides, straight channel solebars and Gloucester floating-axle suspension. However, capacity remained 38 tonnes and they worked side by side with the earlier batch. TAMC 14865 was also recorded at Stoke but in September 1990, when still painted in its original livery.

Centre left: The Great Western main line out of Paddington was host to five privately owned stone terminals belonging to ARC, Bardon, Foster Yeoman, Marcon and Tarmac, while Acton Yard was used as a base for remarshalling stone trains *en route* to other terminals around the capital. On 18 June 1990, having spent the morning at Kensington Olympia, the author took a short Tube ride to Twyford Avenue, arriving just in time to see Class 56 No 56 065 hauling a train of granite from Cliffe Hill to Hayes & Harlington. Included in the formation were various Tarmac PGAs along with a number of former covered hoppers hired from British Industrial Sand. On the down goods a second Class 56 prepares to depart with empty former iron-ore tipplers returning to the ARC quarry at Whatley.

Below left: Tilcon's Swinden Quarry at Rylstone, on the southern fringe of the Yorkshire Dales, also loaded crushed limestone with a daily trainload to either Hull or Leeds and additional runs as required, to Goole. In 1973, the wagon fleet consisted of 33 company-owned PGAs, TCS 14400-32, built by BREL (British Rail Engineering Ltd) at Shildon and a similar number of Charles Roberts-built hoppers hired from Procor. The PGAs owned by Tilcon (Thomas-Tilling Construction) were a unique design having high sides to reduce the risk of fine stone being blown out and pneumatically operated hopper doors.

Following completion of the Humber Bridge and the M62 motorway the extra trains to Goole ceased and the Procor vehicles were no longer required, but in 1987 to cope with an increase in traffic to Leeds, four former salt hoppers were leased and repainted in Wedgwood blue and maroon to match Tilcon's own wagons. On the occasion of a visit by the Railfreight Archive to Rylstone in July 1993, ex-BR shunter No 08 054, itself now in Tilcon colours, had two PGAs in tow: TCS 14432, and nearest the camera, ex-salt PR 8906.

Above and below: In 1994 Tilcon replaced all the two-axle hoppers with 30 French-built JGA 90-tonne-glw bogie wagons leased from Nacco. NACO 19170-99 were fitted with Y25C bogies and, unusually for aggregate hoppers, had hinged top covers to ensure no loss of product *en route*, particularly when running along the environmentally sensitive Rylstone branch itself. In 2001 Tilcon became part of the Tarmac group, and the following year, in addition to their use on the Hull/Leeds circuit, the new wagons began making regular trips to Teesside with limestone for the steel works at Redcar. NACO 19170 was photographed at Rylstone shortly after delivery in April 1994, while NACO 19190 displays the new Tarmac livery at the quarry in May 2001.

2. THE 'BEASTIES'

Left: The British Steel Teesside PGAs, known to local rail staff as the 'Beasties' after their TOPS number prefix, were introduced in 1975 to replace elderly British Rail 25-ton vacuum-braked hoppers on the daily limestone working from Redmire to the blast furnaces at Redcar. Built by Standard Wagon, BSTE 18000-114 were unlike other stone hoppers in having automatic discharge gear and carried 37 tonnes. By 1987 this fleet was gradually being repainted in a mid-grey livery, but BSTE 18047 was still in original condition when noted at Tees Yard that September. Its neighbour, BSTE 18073, was one of 30 that had previously been on hire to ICI for several years to carry rock salt between Over & Wharton in Cheshire and Inverness. The wagons in salt traffic had their top side panels painted red, but all had returned to the Redmire–Redcar circuit by 1986.

Below: Set in delightful Wensleydale, Redmire is a fine spot, although on his last visit the author managed to fall and break his arm! Before the Ministry of Defence took over the site a rather primitive loading platform was used for the stone working as seen in this view dating from September 1991.

Above: At Redmire pairs of empty PGAs were run by gravity from one of the three short holding sidings to the loading chute where end-tipper lorries could dump their load directly into the wagons. A single train of between 20 and 36 wagons normally ran each weekday to Redcar, complete with a brake van so that the guard could close the numerous crossing gates encountered along the branch. However, in 1993, the Redmire working ceased and Hardendale Quarry, near Shap, took over the job of supplying limestone to Redcar. The wagons followed the traffic and BSTE 18028 was photographed beneath the four Matz lime kilns at Hardendale in April 1994.

Below: Until 1992 these hoppers also occasionally carried dolofines from Thrislington Quarry to Redcar, while during the recession of the early 1980s 30 had been sold back to Standard Wagon. Subsequently rebuilt for general mineral traffic with end platforms and ladders, modified door gear and cut-down sides, they were renumbered SRW 18500-29. Ten of the rebuilt PGAs were hired by BR to replace its own ageing HKVs in sand traffic from Redhill to the Crosfield soap factory at Warrington, while a further 12 were used briefly in the agricultural lime traffic from Harrison's Limeworks at Shap Summit to Dumfries. They were also noted carrying rock salt from the Cleveland Potash mine at Boulby to Acton. By 1989, all 30 were back in stone traffic from either Mountsorrel (five PGA), Peak Forest (13 PGA), or Whatley (12 PGA). This late-afternoon view of SRW 18521 (previously BSTE 18056) at Heywood in December 1986 highlights their modified door gear.

3. BOGIE IRON-ORE AND LIMESTONE HOPPERS

Left: In 1953 John Summers & Sons expanded its premises at Shotton in North Wales into a fully integrated steelworks, and instead of using pig iron from its Shelton Works at Etruria it began receiving imported iron ore from Bidston Dock, Birkenhead. That year Charles Roberts completed a batch of 75 46-ton-capacity bogie hopper wagons, and as output increased an additional 48 were constructed in 1958; initially numbered 60-182, on TOPS they became BSSH 13060-182. All were unfitted, so the block trains, whether loaded or empty, were restricted to 35mph between Bidston and Shotton. Furthermore, the severe gradients on the 12½-mile route from the docks to the steelworks limited loaded trains to 11 PHOs plus a brake van and, following the final steam working in November 1967, the workings were entrusted to pairs of BR Type 2 (Class 24) diesel locomotives from Birkenhead Mollington Street. On the odd occasion a Type 4 would substitute, as on a very wet April Fools' Day in 1979, when a Class 47 was photographed rounding the curve at Bidston West Junction with a short formation loaded with Brazilian ore.

Left: Steel production at Shotton ceased in 1980 and the hoppers were then used to move the remaining stockpile of iron ore to Llanwern Steelworks before 103 were sold to ICI. Most were salvaged for spare parts, in particular their plate-back bogies, which ICI wanted, to replace the diamond-frame bogies fitted to many of its similar limestone hoppers. However, 13 of the Shotton wagons were vacuum-braked and after renumbering as ICIM 19152-64 were allocated to the Roadstone pool working from ICI's Tunstead Quarry, near Peak Forest, to the Quick Mix stone terminals at Dean Lane, Manchester, and the Tilcon terminals at Miles Platting and Stockport. In 1987 ICI ceased quarrying at its Hindlow site, south of Buxton, but retained two kilns producing agricultural and industrial lime. To enable production to continue two trains of limestone a day began running from Tunstead and as the demand for roadstone had declined the former Shotton hoppers were transferred to this movement. ICIM 19162 (formerly BSSH 13065) is seen with a load for Hindlow at Great Rocks in March 1991.

Right: ICI's own fleet of 44-ton-capacity bogie hoppers, built in seven batches by Charles Roberts between 1936 and 1953, carried limestone 365 days a year from Tunstead to Northwich for the soda-ash plants set up by Brunner Mond at Lostock and Winnington. Numbered ICIM 19000-151 on TOPS, they were almost six inches taller than the Shotton hoppers and were vacuum-braked from new, although end ladders were fitted only to those in Roadstone traffic and at one end only. In 1992 all the ICI Mond hoppers were re-prefixed 'BLI' to reflect their new ownership by Buxton Lime Industries. In 1998 they were replaced by air-braked stock, but a number were retained at Northwich for the internal movement of coke and limestone, among them BLI 19106 JGV, still going strong at 50 years old, as seen at Oakleigh Sidings, Northwich, on 12 April 1998.

Right: When the venerable ICIM hoppers were withdrawn from main-line use at the end of 1997 a fleet of Procor PGAs, previously leased to ARC and Foster Yeoman, took over the Northwich service, but in 2000 Brunner Mond, by now a separate company again, purchased 27 bogie hoppers from W. H. Davis. BM 19701-6 were built as 'Outers' with conventional buffing gear, while the rest of the fleet, numbered BM 19711-31, were 'Inners' with AAR Type 5 autocouplers. Carrying 76 tonnes each, all run on Nacco swing-motion bogies and the fleet is usually marshalled as a single set of 25 JEAs (three Outers + 19 Inners + three Outers) with two spares for maintenance cover. Up to 12 trains a week run between Tunstead and Northwich although Sunday workings ended in 2005 at the request of Network Rail. BM 19702 brings up the rear of the afternoon departure from Tunstead, passing Great Rocks on 7 July 2002.

Above: Limestone for flue-gas desulphurisation at coal-fired power stations became an increasingly important rail traffic from the Peak District in the 1990s. The first working commenced in 1994 after National Power purchased 21 102-tonne-glw bogie hoppers from Powell Duffryn. Fitted with LTF bogies they ran three or four days a week from Tunstead to Drax Power Station hauled by one of National Power's own Class 59 diesel locomotives. A new depot at Ferrybridge undertook the maintenance of both the motive power and the wagons, and NP 19401 JHA was recorded on site in June 1994.

NP 19400-4 were built as 'Outers' and NP 19405-20 as 'Inners', but at least NP 19403 and NP 19406 swapped roles in later years. In 1998 National Power sold its rail operation to EWS and since then these wagons have worked between the RMC quarry at Doveholes and stone terminals at Acton and Leeds as well as in the revived roadstone trains from Tunstead to Bredbury and Pendleton.

Below left: BTP 24539, a 35-tonner, waits for the next ship to arrive at Immingham in August 1990. Modellers should note that only a handful of wagons received the new Tioxide lettering before the traffic ceased in 1995.

Right: To facilitate the movement of individual wagons to and from repair, BR converted two dozen brake vans into match wagons by fitting them with an auto-coupler at one end. The eight based at Immingham also had their bodywork removed and the then recently recoded BSSC 26006 is seen coupled to two such wagons at Immingham in July 1995.

The rotary coupler end of the wagons was painted orange for easy identification as trains had to be marshalled with all of them facing in the same direction. A number of 'Outer' wagons, fitted with conventional couplings and buffers at one end, were included within each fleet to enable locomotives to be attached. The 'Outer' wagons were of two types: those with a fixed AAR coupler and those with a rotary AAR coupler.

Following the renationalisation of the steel industry in 1967 the British Steel Corporation embarked on a plan to concentrate production at or near coastal sites using imported iron ore from Australia, Canada, Sweden and South America. Rail was chosen to move the ore from the coastal terminals to the nearby steelworks, and as the import berths at Immingham, Redcar, Port Talbot and Hunterston came on stream, separate fleets of 102-tonne-glw bogie tipper wagons were introduced. Relatively cheap to construct and maintain, they overcame the major drawback of the traditional tippler — the need to uncouple each wagon before unloading — through the adoption of AAR auto-couplers, designed to rotate at one end of the wagon. This enabled each vehicle to be tippled whilst still coupled to its neighbours, reducing the time taken to unload an entire train of 21 wagons to less than an hour.

Built at BREL's Shildon works in 1971, the 107 Scunthorpe tipplers were fitted with Y25C bogies whereas all later batches were constructed by Redpath Dorman Long (a BSC subsidiary) in Middlesbrough with BSC's own 'Axle-Motion' bogies. Each wagon carried 75 tonnes of iron ore although given its high density they would often appear to be only half-loaded. Such was the success of the scheme that a schedule of 13 trains a day delivering an impressive 20,475 tonnes was soon introduced between Immingham and Scunthorpe.

4. ILMENITE AND IRON-ORE TIPPLERS

Above: The British Titan Products factory at Grimsby West Marsh processed ilmenite ore into titanium dioxide for use by the paint, paper and ceramics industries. The ilmenite, or black sand, as it is known, was transported by rail from Immingham Dock via the Grimsby Light Railway with an intensive block-train service running whenever a ship arrived, about once a month. In 1950, shortly after the factory opened, BTP purchased 300 former 16-ton cupboard-door mineral wagons from BR and they remained in use until 1974, when W. H. Davis began building a replacement fleet of box-body tipplers on redundant tank-wagon chassis. Allocated TOPS numbers in the range BTP 24300-600 and coded PSO, this new fleet comprised 50 29-tonne and 200 32-tonne vehicles. BTP 24422, identified by its yellow top as a 29-tonner, poses on one of the tipplers at the Grimsby Works in March 1991.

British Steel iron-ore tipplers			
	Inners	*Outers* (non-rotary)	*Outers* (rotary)
BSSC	26000-94	26095-9/105	26100-4/6
BSTE	26450-541	26553-63	26542-52
BSSW	26564-665	26672-7	26666-71
BSRV	26678-778	26790-800	26779-89

Right: Built in 1974, the 114-strong British Steel South Wales batch worked from Port Talbot to Llanwern until steelmaking at Llanwern ceased in 2001. Most repair work on these vehicles was undertaken by BR at Margam, but in August 1991 non-rotary 'Outer' BSSW 26676, together with BSSW 26666, was to be found at Swansea Wagon Works. In 2002 many were sold to the German company VTG for use on short-term flows of aggregates and scrap metals.

Right: Most wide-ranging of all British Steel tipplers were the 123 Ravenscraig wagons built in 1978. Prior to the opening of Hunterston import terminal in 1980 they carried iron ore from the quay at Glasgow General Terminus and coking coal from Rothesay Dock to Ravenscraig Steelworks, near Motherwell. They were also used to deliver limestone from Hardendale Quarry and dolofines from Thrislington Quarry, and although rakes of 21 tipplers were the norm from Hunterston the stone trains were considerably shorter. BSRV 26793 was part of a seven-wagon set seen at Hardendale on 17 May 1992. Like all non-rotary 'Outers' it lacks an orange end.

Above: The 114 British Steel Teesside tipplers introduced in 1973 worked from Redcar to the steelworks at Consett and South Bank. The severe gradients between South Pelaw and Annfield Plain restricted the Consett trains (booked for double-headed Class 37s), to nine wagons, but when Consett closed in 1980 the entire batch was sold to Procor. After fitting ladders and fixing the rotary couplers they were leased by ARC and Foster Yeoman to serve stone terminals not equipped with hopper discharge that had previously relied on railway-owned MSVs. PR 26561 JTA (previously BSTE 26561) was photographed during a visit to the Isle of Grain in April 1993. This was one of 20 JTAs based at Grain for workings to Crawley and Dover, while the rest operated from the Mendips.

Left: Having arrived from Merehead, a train of ex-tipplers, then still coded PTA, is unloaded at Purfleet in May 1985.
courtesy David Mark-Steel

Above: Unlike those leased to Foster Yeoman, where a change of prefix was deemed sufficient, those leased by ARC were also renumbered into the PR 26801-50 series, presumably to provide the company with a consecutive run of numbers. PR 26841 JTA (previously BSTE 26559) gleams in a fresh coat of paint at Stoke in April 1991.

Below: Grab discharge proved to be a very effective method of handling aggregate and when the time came to replace the former iron-ore tipplers Mendip Rail (the joint operating company established by ARC and Foster Yeoman in the mid-1990s) chose to lease a new fleet of 79-tonne-capacity bogie opens from CAIB and Nacco. Numbered NACO 3900-54 and CAIB 3955-89 from 2001 these Mendip Rail wagons took over the workings to terminals at Chichester, Crawley, Exeter, Fareham, Hamworthy, Oxford and Purfleet. NACO 3927 waits to enter traffic having just been completed by Marcroft Engineering at Stoke in October 2000. By this date the CAIB group had acquired both STS and Railcar Services with wagon repair and construction concentrated at Coalville, Gloucester, Stoke and Swansea under the Marcroft Engineering name.

5. CHINA CLAY AND CHALK

Above: China clay is a mica-rich form of granite found in large deposits in Cornwall and Devon. Also known as kaolin, it is used in the manufacture of fine porcelain and to give the lustrous finish to high-quality paper such as used for this book. For many years long-haul traffic from Cornwall to the Potteries, Kent and Scotland was carried in short-wheelbase vacuum-braked five-plank opens, sheeted to protect the clay from the elements, but when BR phased them out in the early 1980s new air-braked designs were introduced.

First off the production line were the 35 'Clay Tigers' developed by English China Clays, British Rail and Tiger Railfreight to carry 57 tonnes of either lump clay (dried clay) or the far stickier ball clay. Introduced in 1982, TRL 11600-34 took over the Potteries traffic with an average of nine or ten PBAs a day being forwarded via Speedlink from various locations in the West Country to a new purpose-built terminal at Stoke Cliffe Vale. The bulk of the clay came from the ECC dries at Parkandillack, Treviscoe, Kernick, Goonbarrow Junction and Marsh Mills with four of the wagons dedicated to carrying ball clay from Heathfield in Devon and Furzebrook, near Wareham in Dorset.

Upon arrival at Stoke a train could be unloaded and on its way back south in around three hours, and with such effective wagon utilisation there was sufficient capacity within the pool for them to also handle ECC clay traffic to Mossend. Given the rapid turnaround it was unusual to find TRL 11617 at Stoke one weekend in March 1991, presumably having been left behind with a mechanical problem. As befits a wagon built in France by Fauvet Girel, it has French Y25C Sambre & Meuse bogies.

Left: Also owned by Tiger Rail were eight two-axle PAA 38-tonne-capacity Covhops leased to the papermakers Tullis Russell. TRL 12800-7 were purpose-built by Standard Wagon in 1981 to negotiate the restricted clearances on the short branch from Markinch to the Tullis Russell mill at Auchmuty. For such a small batch they proved relatively easy to spot being an everyday sight along the West Coast main line. TRL 12804 was found on a visit to Railcar Services' small works at Gloucester in April 1987.

Right: In 1989 Tullis Russell leased a ninth Covhop from Tiger, TRL 12300. This vehicle, also coded PAA, had originally been DAVS 14433, a 51-tonne-glw aggregate hopper built by W. H. Davis at the height of the construction boom, in anticipation of attracting future orders which never came. It languished in store at Shirebrook for over a decade until being fitted with new discharge doors and a top-cover for its new role. This photograph of TRL 12300 was taken at St Blazey (never an easy yard to get around) during a group visit in 1992. Most of the china clay transported by rail to Auchmuty originated from Goonbarrow Junction, near Bugle, but there were also occasional loads from Burngullow and Drinnick Mill. Unfortunately, having survived the demise of Speedlink the Tullis Russell traffic was a casualty of the collapse of Tiger Rail, and the wagons were withdrawn after only 10 years' service.

Left: To supply the Wiggins Teape paper mill at Corpach, just outside Fort William, another new type was introduced in 1983. As Corpach was not equipped for hopper unloading Railease converted 14 high-sided 38-tonne PMV mineral wagons fitting them with air brakes, ladders, inspection platforms and a removable roller roof. Coded PRA, RLS 6303-16 ran almost exclusively between the small ECC dries at Pontsmill, near St Blazey, and Corpach although at least one wagon is known to have carried a load of china clay from Drinnick Mill to P. D. Stirling at Mossend. RLS 6308 was spotted passing Warrington Bank Quay in September 1984. In 1989 the mill at Corpach changed to using clay slurry delivered in tank wagons and the PRAs went into store.

Right: Built at Heywood in 1971 to carry salt from Middlewich to the BP Chemicals plant at Baglan Bay, the 55 46-tonne-glw 'Baby Salts' lasted less than four years with BP before being replaced by a fleet of 51-tonners. Subsequently, PR 8201-55 were used in several seasonal traffics including agricultural lime from Coxhoe to Brechin and rock salt from Over & Wharton to Exeter. Six of the PGAs were leased by Electro-Furnace Products to carry aluminium oxide from its works at Hull Docks to Universal Abrasives at Stafford for use in the manufacture of grindstones, while P. D. Stirling leased four wagons (PR 8212/42/5/51) for clay traffic. Most loadings comprised ball clay from Watts Blake Bearne at Newton Abbot, but on 28 March 1989 PR 8212 had just arrived at Mossend with 33 tons of china clay from the splendidly named Goonvean & Rostowrack Clay Co siding at Carbis Wharf, Bugle, Cornwall.

Above: The Bowaters train, used to convey china-clay slurry from the ECC plant at Burngullow to Sittingbourne, comprised 18 tanks, STS 53111-28 on TOPS, built in 1967 by Rootes Pressings (Scotland) Ltd at Linwood. As china clay is very susceptible to contamination the tank barrels had an 'Epimastic' lining with glassfibre insulation beneath the outer cladding to protect the slurry from freezing. Two additional tanks, STS 53119/20 were built by IMC at Hartlepool in 1971, and all 20 TTAs had a tare of 13 tons and a payload of 32 tons.

In the early 1970s the Bowaters tanks were repainted and lost their company logo, but they continued to supply the paper mill at Sittingbourne, which from 1985 also began receiving calcium carbonate slurry from the ECC works at Quidhampton. Tanks from Quidhampton were routed via Severn Tunnel Junction (STJ), where they could join a direct Speedlink to Hoo Junction — which explains the inclusion of STS 53116 and STS 53115 at the head of an Eastleigh–Severn Tunnel Junction freight seen passing through Westbury in March 1986.

Left: A decline in the use of heavy chemicals resulted in many tank wagons becoming surplus, and both 46- and 51-tonne caustic soda tanks were transferred to slurry traffic. TRL 70705, a TUA previously operated by ICI, was one of a dozen leased by ECC in 1988 to transport china-clay slurry between Burngullow and Aberdeen Guild Street and was photographed at Warrington Arpley in July 1990.

Above: Joseph Crosfield & Sons' soap works at Warrington was another important destination for clay slurry in the years prior to the end of Speedlink. Five 59-tonne capacity bogie Tiger TCAs, TRL 78800-4, built by CFMF in 1975 originally to carry sulphuric acid for Leathers Chemicals, were converted to carry china clay slurry in 1981 and worked to Warrington from Burngullow and Newton Abbot until 1987, when they were repainted in ECC livery and reallocated to Quidhampton. TRL 78804 was recorded outside Crosfield's at Warrington in January 1987.

Below: As replacements for the TCAs Tiger drafted in nine redundant caustic soda tanks, four TTAs and five TUAs, although none would be repainted in Crosfield's livery before the traffic ended in 1991. TRL 70724 came from the Standard-built batch, TRL 70700-27, originally operated by ICI. Aside from having a grey patch over the ICI roundel it was in original (albeit slurry-stained) condition when photographed under a threatening sky at Warrington on Christmas Eve 1989.

Left: Crosfield's TTAs were taken from a large batch, TRL 51586-648, built by Charles Roberts back in 1967, again for ICI. Resprung and repainted black, TRL 51635 was found amongst the weeds outside the soap works at Warrington in July 1990.

Below: Arguably the best-known freight service in recent years has been the twice-weekly block train of china clay slurry from Burngullow to the Caledonian Paper mill at Irvine in south-west Scotland. The train began running in 1989 and quickly became known as the 'Silver Bullet', a reference to the 67.5-tonne capacity internationally registered stainless steel bogie tanks built for the working by ANF Industries. Those tanks, which will be discussed in the author's forthcoming volume on ferry wagons, were replaced in 2002 by NACO 89100-29, thirty 102-tonne-glw vehicles capable of carrying an extra 11 tonnes. The new tanks also took over the chalk-slurry traffic from Quidhampton to Sittingbourne and to the Iggesund paperboard mill at Workington. NACO 89103 was still relatively clean when spotted at Warrington in June 2003.

Above: Paper makers also use imported chalk slurry from Norway and in 1988 Croxton & Garry leased four former Class B TUAs (PR 70079/83/5/9) to work between Aberdeen Waterloo Goods and Sittingbourne. All four were repainted, and PR 70089 was recorded when on exhibition at Coalville in June 1989.

Left: Croxton & Garry also purchased eight former bogie cement Presflos from Blue Circle which were converted at Stoke to carry chalk slurry. They also worked from Aberdeen and regular destinations included Blackburn and Workington in addition to Sittingbourne. CG 9743 coded JCA was at Fogarty's distribution depot at Blackburn on 28 July 1997 with 79 tonnes of slurry destined for a wallpaper mill in Darwen.

Right: Bagged china clay was also transported by rail although predominantly in railway-owned or internationally registered vans. However, TRL 6950, the unique 29-tonne-capacity curtain-sided 'Railiner' was briefly used on workings from Par Harbour and Pontsmill to Ashford and Mossend. Built by C. C. Crump in 1981 on the underframe of cyclohexane tank TRL 51915, the PVA was spotted at St Blazey in August 1987.

6. LIME AND DOLIME

Left: Lime is used as a flux in steel making, and in 1972 British Steel leased sixty-nine 46-tonne-glw covered hoppers from BRTE to supply its steelworks in the North East. Initially BRTE 8050-8118 were loaded at Tilcon's Rylstone Quarry, to form a daily block train of 26 PAAs running to either Consett or Lackenby as required, but after the closure of Consett they began working from Hardendale to Lackenby. Built by Standard Wagon at Heywood, the BRTE Covhops carried 33 tonnes of lime, and BRT 8115 was spotted in typically work-stained condition at Hardendale in May 1992.

Below: Hardendale Quarry was also the originating point for lime traffic to Ravenscraig, for which a batch of fifty 37-tonne capacity, 51-tonne-glw Covhops was built at BREL's Ashford Works in 1974. Owned by British Steel Glasgow, BSGL 8050-99 were considerably longer than the BRTE wagons, having a 20ft 3in wheelbase compared with 16ft. In place of three hinged roof-hatches they were fitted with a one-piece roof cover which allowed for quicker loading and at the same time reduced the risk of water contamination. When they were ordered it had been planned that these wagons would also supply the Clydebridge steelworks at Rutherglen, but this was subsequently selected for closure. In 1993 these PAAs, commonly known as the 'White Ladies' after their dusty appearance, replaced the BRTE Covhops in the Lackenby circuit and in 2004 they were purchased by EWS.

BSGL 8199 stands at Hardendale in May 1993 while in the background only two of the four gas-fired kilns appear to be in action. In the 1980s, two trains of butane arrived each week from Stanlow oil refinery to power the kilns but by the date of this visit only outgoing lime and limestone were still on rail.

Right: Until 1983 the steelworks at Scunthorpe had received lime from Steetley Quarry, at Hindlow, but when that flow ceased the fifty 46-tonne-glw Covhops built for the traffic at Heywood in 1970, PR 8000-49, were transferred to other workings. Twenty-five of the PABs were modified with new top hatches and leased by British Aluminium to transport imported alumina from Invergordon, and from 1984 Blyth, to the smelter at Fort William, while of the remainder 15 went to Steetley's Thrislington Quarry at Ferryhill, the rest staying at Hindlow. An early morning visit to Ashbury's finds one of the shunters struggling with the brake lever on PR 8008 during a spot of loose shunting at the West Sidings on 10 July 1985. PR 8008 was one of three empty PABs *en route* to Hindlow to collect another load of glassworks limestone for the P. D. Stirling distribution depot at Mossend.

Left: PR 8008 was subsequently transferred to Thrislington and in May 1991 the author encountered it again awaiting repair outside the Steetley Magnesia Works at Hartlepool Cemetery Point. Here lime and dolime (calcined dolomite, a magnesium-rich form of calcium carbonate), brought by rail from Thrislington, were used in the extraction of magnesium from seawater. The factory had been built in 1937 with governmental assistance as the country prepared for war.

Right: Since the 1950s both minerals had been carried in BR 20-ton Covhops, but in 1981, Steetley was awarded a Section 8 grant to purchase new wagons. Thirty distinctive 51-tonne-glw covered hoppers, fitted with air-operated top covers, were built by Standard Wagon for the dolime traffic and numbered STET 18700-29. These PAAs were also long vehicles at 25ft 7in over headstocks with a 19ft wheelbase and carried 36 tonnes. The large side panels were fitted to facilitate shunting by Hymid Wagon Controllers at Thrislington. The type rarely strayed from the North East as all routine maintenance was handled at Thornaby and this view of STET 18703 was taken at Tees Yard in February 1992, shortly after a visit to the adjacent wagon shop.

Above: At Hartlepool Steetley produced magnesia and sintered magnesite for the steel, glass and ceramics industries and in earlier days these had also been conveyed by rail, but by 1991 the internal rail system only handled incoming traffic. One of the two industrial locomotives at the works was in daily use tripping wagons to and from the BR exchange sidings at Cemetery North and shunting within the plant. On 6 June 1992 Hudswell Clarke D1346, an 0-4-0DH, hauls Covhops through the discharge house.

Below: On 28 September 1991 Steetley's other locomotive, Hunslet 7425, also an 0-4-0 diesel-hydraulic, shunts empty lime wagons in the small, three-road yard within the works. Situated on the headland to the east of the town, with the North Sea immediately behind the buildings in the background, the magnesia works could be an uncomfortable spot particularly on a wet and windy day such as this. Nonetheless it was a fascinating place and it was a pity that it eventually fell victim to cheap imports and increased environmental concerns in 2004.

7. A VARIETY OF VANS

Left: Built in 1956 the cupboard-door Palvans were not a success on BR, as continued loading caused excessive wear, making them unstable at speed, and they were destined to have relatively short lives. However, they were adequate for the restricted task required of them by John Walker & Sons, which, in 1967, purchased 20 vans from British Rail to carry casks of blended whisky from its blending plant at Barleith to its bottling plant four miles away at Kilmarnock High Street. Other than being repainted and renumbered as JW 6050-69 they were unmodified apart from advertisement boards added to the sides and remained in whisky traffic until 1981, when a new blending plant opened at Kilmarnock. Subsequently the PVVs were donated to preservation societies at Bridge of Dun, Bo'ness and Dalmellington and JW 6057 was one of three photographed during a visit to Bo'ness in May 1993; a trip also memorable for the Norwegian cod in batter served at the nearby Blackness Inn. It was numbered B773039 by BR; the 'CLV 204' beneath the advertisement board was its Johnnie Walker fleet number, CLV referring to a Crown Lockfast Vehicle, and a common marking on all vehicles allocated to whisky traffic under the supervision of HM Customs & Excise.

Below: Food and drink were also the preserve of the 15 Campbell's Soup vans built by Standard Wagon in 1973. BRT 6900-14 carried tinned foodstuffs from the Campbell's factory at King's Lynn to the NCL depot at Leith Walk in Edinburgh and to Glasgow High Street goods depot until 1982, when all traffic was transferred to a new private terminal opened by Corylink at Law Junction, near Motherwell. At the same time eight vans, BRT 6900/4-7/11/3/4, had their four wooden sliding doors each side replaced by full-length curtains, a modification designed to overcome the main problem encountered with the original vehicles — that of loads shifting in transit, jamming the sliding doors.

Emblazoned with the company name, the modified Campbell's vans often featured in BR literature advertising the virtues of the Speedlink network, and in 1987 the PVBs also began working to the Stockton Haulage terminal at Stranraer Town. BRT 6913 was found back at Horbury awaiting repair in November 1988.

To meet the additional demands placed on its wagon fleet by the Stranraer traffic in 1987 Campbell's also leased two Procor curtain-sided vans built in 1982. At 41ft 9in these were 7ft longer than the BRT vans and as more became available for hire the shorter vehicles were gradually removed from service.

Left: In addition to soup the 20 Procor PVAs, PR 6915-34, were used to transport various commodities, notably bagged fertiliser from Middlesbrough and Ince & Elton on behalf of ICI and UKF respectively. Palletised patent fuel blocks from the Homefire plant at Three Spires, Coventry were another source of traffic, being transported to TCFD (Tyneside Central Freight Depot) at Gateshead, while in 1986 two vans were hired by Clyde Cement to move bagged cement from its Sunnyside works at Coatbridge to Aberdeen and Dundee. Another short-term hire in 1987 saw a single van carrying Anchor roof tiles between Wolverton and Rochester.

From November 1985 Rugby Cement leased five of the PVAs (PR 6917/31-4) to transport bagged cement to Ardwick West Freight Depot in Manchester where PR 6931 was photographed on New Year's Day 1986. The cement originated at a Rugby Cement plant near Scunthorpe but the working was anything but intensive as, without any warehousing at Ardwick, the vans were used for short-term storage. For example, a visit to Ardwick on 5 April 1986 found three loaded vans at the depot, none having arrived more recently than 20 March, and one was still at Ardwick a fortnight later, only half unloaded.

Left: Singled out for special treatment was PR 6917, which had new curtains fitted for its trip to the Railfreight Exhibition at Cricklewood in March 1989, being seen here on its return to Horbury in May; later that year it went into Campbell's Soup traffic, complete with CAIB curtains.

Left: In 1976 Procor built PR 6400, a unique 35ft-long pallet van designed to provide full access for loading and unloading. This was achieved by forming each side from a combination of four small cupboard-doors with sliding panels located between each pair of doors. The two central doors were hinged to the adjacent panel, so that when opened they formed a single sliding unit, and by opening the doors and sliding the panels in various ways it was possible to access one-half of the side, or to produce a central opening some 17ft 3in wide.

Right: Procor's design showed great ingenuity but it had few if any advantages over British Rail's own air-braked vans. After early trials with W. M. Cory & Sons PR 6400 was leased to Ben Chairs (Western) Ltd of Frome, Somerset, to carry contract furniture (for pubs, clubs, hotels, conference centres etc) to the more distant parts of the country and destinations visited by the PVB included Glasgow High Street, Norwich and TCFD. Unfortunately the inherent weakness in the van's sides saw it damaged twice while passing other trains in the Severn Tunnel which led to all but one of the doors being permanently closed. The resultant limited access led to numerous breakages when unloading large items of furniture and by February 1987 the Ben Chairs van was out of use at Horbury Junction.

Left: UKF Fertilisers owned over 90 bogie Palvans built by the Gloucester Railway Carriage & Wagon Co, BREL Ashford, Procor and W. H. Davis between 1968 and 1975 to carry bagged fertiliser from its compound fertiliser plant at Ince & Elton in Cheshire. Amongst the vans' unique features were an intermediate floor, to make full use of their 48-tonne capacity, internal bulkheads and dunnage bags, to prevent the load from moving in transit, and smooth aluminium facing to all internal surfaces, to protect the plastic bags of fertiliser from being ripped during loading or unloading. The first 30 vans, LS 7001-30, were built with curtain-sides but these were later replaced by four pairs of cupboard-doors per side to match the rest of the fleet. The PWAs ran in block trains and wagonload services to dedicated fertiliser storage depots and general goods yards throughout the country. SSTR 7309, one of the final batch built by Procor in 1976, waits to be unloaded at Banbury in April 1989.

Right: Although a great success, with eight doors each side, the fertiliser vans were prone to damage from fork-lift trucks and eventually 12 vans were rebuilt by W. H. Davis with new doors and a flat roof. Following the Kemira takeover of UKF in 1989 a few vans were repainted in the new livery, but when the traffic ended in 1993 the majority were still painted brown and white, albeit with the large UKF logo having been painted out. Rebuilt LS 7007 was spotted in the carriage & wagon sidings at Warrington in July 1990.

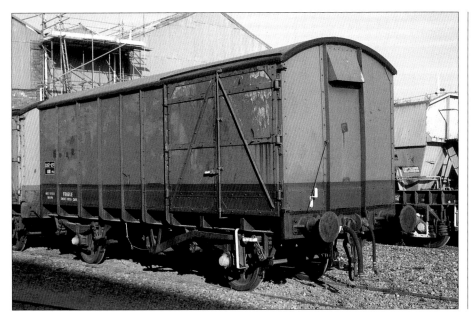

8. MILITARY MANOEUVRES

Left: All three services of the Armed Forces used rail to move supplies and equipment to their depots throughout the country. Much of this traffic went in railway-owned vans and opens, but in 1968 the Gloucester Railway Carriage & Wagon Co built a batch of 16ft-wheelbase Palvans for the Ministry of Defence: MODA 6800-15. All but two of these PVBs were withdrawn from main-line use in 1982, but MODA 6804 and 6811 were retained, specifically to carry re-railing equipment to the scene of any derailment within a military installation. MODA 6804 was based at Longtown, and MODA 6811 (seen at Stoke awaiting repair in October 1999) at Marchwood.

Above: The MoD purchased 27 two-axle curtain-sided vans from CAIB in 1998. Seven were former Campbell's Soup vans which were renumbered MODA 7420-6, while the remainder comprised the former Procor batch, PR 6915-34, which became MODA 7427-46. MODA 7428 (ex-PR 6916), now coded PMA, was in the exchange sidings at Bicester Ordnance Depot in May 1999.

Left: Since the early 1990s military traffic has increasingly been moved in containers on both railway and privately owned conflats with container terminals set up at Bicester, Eastriggs, Kineton, Longtown and Marchwood. On 10 September 1992 TIPH 93365, loaded with three Royal Corps of Transport 20ft boxes, is shunted into the exchange sidings at Bicester by one of the Army's 335hp Thomas Hill 'Steelman' locomotives, No 272 *Royal Pioneer.*

Above and below: The 82-tonne-glw Tiphook flats were built in two batches by Rautaruukki of Finland: TIPH 93242-81 in 1987 with Gloucester pedestal-suspension bogies, and TIPH 93290-489 in 1988 with Sambre-et-Meuse bogies, all being recoded from PFA to KFA in 1991.

In addition to conventional containers they handled more unusual military loads; in September 2002 TIPH 93357 was recorded at Bicester with 20ft cabins, while TIPH 93243 was one of several carrying 20ft Flatracks at Didcot in May 2001.

Left: In 1995 the MoD purchased the 40 two-axle conflats built by Procor to carry Kelly coal containers. Re-prefixed 'MODA', a few were repainted in Army green, but MODA 93225 PFA retained its original livery at Bicester in April 1997. Between 1998 and 2000 they were hired by British Gypsum and carried containers of disulphogypsum from Southampton Docks to their works at East Leake and Mountfield, but by 2001 all had returned to military service.

Right: To transport vehicles and larger items of equipment the MoD operated 125 air-braked Warwells and Warflats. Built in the 1940s the Warwells were originally fitted with diamond-frame bogies and vacuum brakes but in 1976 60 (MODA 95500-48/73-83) were refurbished with air brakes and Gloucester pedestal suspension bogies, while a new batch of 65 Warflats (MODA 95233-97) was built at BREL's Shildon Works. Both types can carry 51 tonnes and at 43ft long are able to negotiate the tightly curved sidings found at many military depots. Back in the days of Speedlink these wagons would often turn up with unusual loads, and this view of MODA 95545, coded PFB, at Warrington Walton Old Junction in August 1987 carrying a Baguley-Drewry railcar, is one of the author's favourites. Army No AD 9129 was being transferred from the Proof & Experimental Establishment at Shoeburyness to the Vickers gun range at Eskmeals.

Left: Didcot has been an important centre for MoD trains with a daily trunk working to Carlisle and trips to Ashchurch, Bicester, Kineton and Marchwood. On 8 September 1991 MODA 95543 was one of five Warwells each loaded with a Land Rover field ambulance awaiting delivery to the Central Vehicle Depot at Ashchurch the following day. Note the integral headstock-mounted screw-jacks, which could be screwed down to rail height for stability when vehicles were being driven on and off.

Right: Donnington Central Ordnance Depot in Shropshire was one of the locations that lost its rail service in 1991 having previously been served by an extension of the Bescot–Wellington Speedlink. On a visit to Wellington in October 1986 the author arrived at the station to find the return Speedlink stabled in one of the centre roads, waiting to be overtaken by a Shrewsbury–Euston InterCity train. In addition to several railway-owned vans the freight included MODA 95505, one of three Warwells loaded with these small containers used by the Army for command and communications in the field.

Above and right: In 1996 the MoD began moving armoured fighting vehicles between Redmire and Ludgershall by rail, the AFVs being *en route* from Catterick Garrison to Salisbury Plain. Warwell MODA 95504, now coded KWB, carries a Samaritan at Redmire on 19 September 1999 while earlier that month, MODA 95241, coded KFB, headed a rake of Warflats loaded with Spartans and Scimitars. *courtesy Mark Saunders (both)*

Left: Armoured vehicles were also transported by rail from Donnington, Shropshire, such as these three Ferret scout cars loaded on MODA 95268, coded PFB, recorded at Bescot in July 1984.

Below: Didcot was overdue a visit from the weedkilling train as MODA 95274, coded KFB, waits to leave for Ashchurch with a Land Rover and four Sankey wide-track trailers *en route* from Marchwood Military Port in September 1991.

Bottom: Prior to the introduction of the Shildon-built batch the MoD had operated over 100 vacuum-braked Warflats in main-line service. Numbered MODA 95105-230 and coded PFV on TOPS, many were retained for internal use including MODA 95138, seen at Bicester Graven Hill in July 2000 carrying 46 new tyres.

Above and below: The MoD also owned one of the giants of the wagon world, MODA 95780, the 'Hot Core'. Built in 1963 this 188-ton monster ran on two 12-wheeled bogies and moved spent nuclear submarine cores from the naval shipyards at Chatham, Devonport and Rosyth to Sellafield for reprocessing. The cores were carried in a special flask slung between the wagon's massive side frames and when loaded ran as a special train accompanied by a contingent of military police and dockyard workers who travelled in two escort coaches converted from BR Mk 1 BSKs and renumbered MODA 99150 and 99151. The 'Hot Core' was built by Head Wrightson with vacuum brakes and was initially coded PXV but had been air-braked by the time this photograph was taken at Carlisle Currock wagon shop on a rather dull day in September 1993. By April 1995 the escort coaches had been replaced by railway-owned inspection saloons and both were in store at Bicester.

9. CEMENT

Above left: British Railways had identified powdered materials as a source of potential new business soon after Nationalisation and in 1954 introduced the 20-ton Presflo. This revolutionary design was intended to overcome the problems inherent in carrying cement in bulk and incorporated two top-filling hatches for rapid and even loading and, most crucial of all, a system of air-assisted discharge. Cement, unlike many other powdered loads, does not flow easily, while vibration during transit causes it to compact, so that unloading from a conventional hopper becomes very time-consuming. However, pumping compressed air into the wagon changes the fluidity of the cement such that it will flow like a liquid and can easily be discharged into trackside silos or similarly equipped road tankers.

As the postwar rebuilding boom gathered pace BR built nearly 2,000 Presflos, uprating the capacity to 22 tons, and in 1960 both Associated Portland Cement and Tunnel Cement purchased their own examples from the Butterley Wagon Co. Numbered TC 8951-8, the Tunnel PCVs carried special sulphate-resisting cement from the Aberthaw Cement company at Rhoose and from Tunnel's own Pitstone works, near Tring, to a terminal in Southampton. When new, the company name and logo were painted on a large rectangular board fixed to the side, but by 1980 these were painted directly on the wagons. This view of TC 8955 at Pitstone in November 1981 illustrates the complicated pipework which was fitted to one side only of these Presflos.

Centre left: Unlike other major cement companies, which purchased their own wagons, Ketton Cement leased a fleet of 38-tonne-capacity depressed-centre PCAs from Tiger Railcar Leasing. TRL 9460-74 were built at BREL's Doncaster Works in 1975 and ran as a block train from Ketton to a new cement terminal at Castle Bromwich. From 1982 they began working, together with other Tiger PCAs leased by Ketton, in Speedlink to Bletchley, Portishead, Sheffield and Wymondham. Only the original batch was painted in an attractive green livery, complete with the company name, but Ketton seems to have had equally as much difficulty in keeping its wagons clean. TRL 9469 was in typical condition for a wagon that had been in traffic for a few months when noted at Marcroft's works in Coalville in June 1989.

Left: Following a shake-up in the cement industry Ketton, Ribble and Tunnel became part of Castle Cement, and in 1996 the older air-braked stock at Ketton made way for 67 French built PCAs dating from the 1980s. Built by CFMF and fitted with 'Powderjet Fluidization' the recently arrived STS 10600 was recorded at Ketton in August 1996. In 2004 this fleet was sold to VTG, becoming VTG 10600-51 and VTG 74030-44.

Above and right: In the 1970s a number of different cylindrical pressure-discharge designs were introduced including a batch of 36 powder tanks built in 1972 by Installation Manufacturing Contractors at Hartlepool for Tunnel Cement. TC 8983-9018 were air-braked with pedestal suspension and carried 39 tonnes, a significant improvement on the earlier design. When new they went into traffic from Tring conveying ordinary cement to Kings Cross and Southampton and after Tring closed in 1991 began working between Ketton and King's Cross. Coded PCA, they were painted in an overall red livery, with a large Tunnel logo in white and the company name in black lettering, but only the slightest trace of red was discernible when I photographed TC 8995 being propelled, along with several STS ferry-registered Twin-Silo wagons, into the exchange sidings at Tring in May 1988. Unfortunately they were no cleaner when working from Ketton, as evident from this view of the non-ladder end of TC 9017, recorded outside the works in September 1991.

Above: Rugby Cement, with a number of relatively small flows from its plants at Foxton, Halling, Rugby and South Ferriby (near Scunthorpe) contributed around 15% of rail-borne cement traffic. The bulk of its wagon fleet comprised 81 37-tonne-capacity 'Pressure Flow' PCAs, built at Horbury Junction between 1973 and 1981, of which 28 were used to carry cement from Scunthorpe Freight Depot to Stapleford & Sandiacre. This pool also supplied Ardwick Goods in Manchester, and on 5 April 1986 RC 10025 was one of five PCAs at the depot. Five or six wagons a week were normally sent to Ardwick, but with limited static storage there they often remained for some days before being unloaded.

Below: Rugby Cement traffic ceased in 1990, and the PCAs went into store until 2001, when 15 were refurbished to carry powdered lime mortar from the Ready Mix Concrete works at Peak Forest. RC 10025 was amongst those refurbished, and 20 years on the author caught up with it again at Peak Forest, where on 13 July 2006 it was bringing up the rear of a train of empties returning from Bletchley.

Above: Rugby also owned 15 PCAs built by Procor in 1984 to a hybrid design which combined the Charles Roberts 'Pressure Flow' with a sloping barrel floor. All worked from Foxton to Bow and Norwich, but by September 1993 RC 10060 was in store at Foxton with the rest of the batch

Below: In 1999 RC 10050-64 were purchased by EWS, eight being renumbered and recoded CSA before a return to traffic the following year carrying lime from the Buxton Lime Company kilns at Hindlow to the recently reopened Uskmouth Power Station, near Newport. The lime was used in flue-gas desulphurisation at the power station, which its new owner, AES Electric, had renamed Fifoots Point. However, market conditions within the generating industry soon turned against AES, and the station closed again in early 2002. The CSAs then went to Jake Rail Tank Cleaning Services at Ellesmere Port for cleaning, and on 8 July 2002 all eight could be found lined up in the overgrown run-round loop outside the small works.

Above: Sodium tripolyphosphate (STPP), the main constituent of powdered detergent, was manufactured by Albright & Wilson in its Marchon Works at Corkickle, near Whitehaven, and transported to soap factories at Port Sunlight, Warrington and West Thurrock. In 1982 the remaining BR Prestwin wagons in this traffic were withdrawn after Lever Bros leased 12 new 37-tonne-capacity depressed-centre PCAs from Tiger Rail. Built by Standard Wagon, TRL 10522-33 ran in wagonload freights, although workings to Port Sunlight ended in 1984 when Lever Bros concentrated detergent production in Warrington. Four wagons a day were required to supply the 'Persil' plant, these being detached from the overnight Workington–Dover Speedlink in Warrington Arpley Yard and shunted in to Lever Bros early the next morning. TRL 10525 is seen entering the factory at Warrington on 20 July 1985.

Below: Until October 1986 the PCAs were loaded within the Marchon Works but once the rope-worked incline at Corkickle closed the wagons were modified for side loading from road lorries at Whitehaven Preston Street goods depot. Despite the efficiency of the rail operation, which saw some wagons making three loaded journeys a week, Lever Bros abandoned rail in 1990, and shortly thereafter the PCAs were transferred to the West Thurrock service. Most were repainted in Albright & Wilson livery, but TRL 10522/3 gained a new blue scheme while TRL 10524/5 remained in purple minus the Lever Bros logo. TRL 10522 was captured at Whitehaven on 9 May 1992. Note the loading valve fitted at Crump's just above the solebar near the centre line of the body.

Right: Six additional purple PCAs, TRL 10534-9, built for Tiger Rail in 1982 and leased to Ketton Cement, were also added to the West Thurrock STPP pool in 1989. TRL 10538, fresh from a repaint at Crump's, was at Warrington that October.

Below: STPP for the Procter & Gamble factory at West Thurrock, the home of 'Ariel' and 'Daz', began arriving in air-braked private-owner wagons in 1972, when Charles Roberts built a fleet of 13 102-tonne-glw, 71-tonne-capacity bogie powder tanks. PR 11300-12, coded PBA, joined a prototype (CL 84701) constructed three years earlier, running as a Fridays-only block train from Whitehaven until July 1977, when six of the wagons were written off when the train derailed at Braystones, on the Cumbrian coast.

Procor provided as replacements 12 PCAs from the PR 10000-18 batch. Built in 1976, primarily for cement, they were not ideal for STPP, and in 1983 a new fleet of 16 depressed-centre PCAs fitted with Gloucester floating-axle suspension, PR 9494-9 and 10125-34, replaced both them and the surviving PBAs. PR 10134 awaits loading at Whitehaven in May 1992. The increasing cost of rail, combined with the decision to run down the works at Corkickle, resulted in the demise of the STPP traffic in 1994.

Above and below: After the newer PCAs took over the West Thurrock service two of the redundant powder wagons were sent to Manchester to be evaluated by the Corn Product Co for possible future use on starch traffic.

PR 11300 and PR 10011 were recorded at Ardwick on 24 February 1985. The vertical bands on the PBA were painted white but over the years weathered to this yellow shade.

Top: Evidently the trials were a success for in 1986 the eight remaining PBAs, PR 11300/4-6/8/9/11/2, were repainted in CPC livery and began moving bulk starch to the paper mills at Aberdeen, Corpach, Port Elphinstone and Sittingbourne. PR 11304 awaits loading in Ardwick West Goods in March 1986 as a train of Peakstone hoppers slips past in the distance on the line to Phillips Park Junction.

Above: This livery was another favourite of the author' but it proved short lived for two years later CPC became part of Cerestar and the wagons were repainted once again. PR 11308 shows off the new look at Trafford Park in March 1994.

Right: Loading had been moved to the company's factory in Trafford Park in 1989, shortly after the reopening of the Trafford Park Estate Co's internal rail system, and to cope with increased traffic Cerestar leased 15 of the PCAs, PR 10000-3/5-11/3/4/7/8. PR 10006 is seen at Trafford Park in April 1994.

11. SODA ASH

Left: Sodium carbonate, often referred to as soda ash, has been manufactured by Brunner Mond in Northwich since the 1870s, and by 1970 the works at Lostock, Wallerscote and Winnington, then owned by ICI, were producing one million tons a year. Much of this output was transported by rail, using BR 20-ton Covhops, to end users in the glass, detergent and chemical industries.

The first air-braked private-owner wagons built for soda ash were the 60 unique 43-tonne-glw 'Tip-Air' tanks introduced in 1975. Carrying 26 tonnes of light soda ash (used in the manufacture of soap powder), RLS 12200-59 worked from the ICI works at Lostock to Albright & Wilson at Corkickle. To accomplish discharge of this lightweight material the wagon's pressure-discharge tank body was mounted on a special underframe fitted with a pneumatic ram at one end thus allowing the tank to be tilted to provide a sloping bed during unloading. When new RLS 12200 was coded TEB, while the rest were coded TEA, these being redesignated PEB and PEA respectively in 1981. Although a success, the Tip-Airs were of little use to other customers and were withdrawn once the internal railway at Corkickle closed. RLS 12200 was one of several stored out of use at Heywood in November 1988.

All 60 underframes were eventually reused; 20 had low-sided box bodies fitted for aggregate traffic, becoming RLS 5234-53, and the remainder were converted in two batches into POA scrap opens for Allied Steel & Wire, becoming RLS 4560-79 and RLS 5214-33. The underframe from RLS 12200 became the basis of RLS 4562.

Centre left: ICI also leased 40 PCAs to carry heavy soda ash from its works at Wallerscote and Winnington to a distribution depot at Larbert, from where it was taken by road to customers in Scotland's central belt. Built by Procor, they were conventional 51-tonne-glw powder wagons with a payload of 37 tonnes. PR 9475-84, built 1976, were fitted with BSC friction-pedestal suspension, while PR 10100-24, built 1980, had Gloucester floating-axle suspension. In the Speedlink era these vehicles also ran occasionally to distribution depots at Ely and Willesden, but by April 1993, when the author recorded PR 10107 in Oakleigh Sidings, Northwich, only the block-train service to Scotland survived, and that too was to cease two months later.

Left: Heavy soda ash for the Rockware Glass factories at Barnby Dun and Knottingley was also conveyed by Speedlink, in a batch of Tiger Rail PCAs built at Shildon in 1983. TRL 10540-69 differed from earlier depressed-centre types in having a conical end-vessel strake, which better suited the settling properties of soda ash. Following the closure of the glassworks in Knottingley TRL 10540-5 were hired by Minworth Metals to transport barytes from Mossend to Aberdeen and Lowestoft, while TRL 10568/9 were transferred to Ketton Cement before ending their days in STPP traffic from Corkickle. After a couple of years in store at Northwich TRL 10540-67 were cut up at Stockton in 1993. In happier days, in April 1985, TRL 10552 was spotted at Oakleigh Sidings.

12. BREAD AND BUTTER

Right: The BRTE bulk-grain vans built in the mid-1960s for the Distillers and Associated British Maltsters Anglo-Scottish barley traffic were amongst the most recognisable of private-owner wagons. At the time of their construction their 28-ton payload was a significant improvement on BR's own 20-ton hoppers, and their blue (Distillers) or yellow (ABM) body colour made these vacuum-braked wagons popular prototypes with model manufacturers. However, by 1980, having run intensively up and down the East Coast main line for well over a decade, most were on their last legs, and when Distillers purchased replacement bogie Polybulks in 1982 the majority of the 'Blues', as the PAFs were known, went into store.

BRT 7766, seen awaiting disposal at Railcar Services, Stoke, in June 1985, came from the final batch of 55 PAFs, built at BREL Doncaster in 1971 with pedestal suspension. Until 1977 many of these wagons had carried on their sides large boards displaying colourful transfers advertising different brands of whisky, although it is uncertain whether all this batch were so adorned, despite having the necessary fixing brackets.

Right: In 1984, 35 from the last batch of bulk grain vans were refurbished, air-braked and leased to Traffic Services Ltd. Referred to as Minibulks, they were employed chiefly to supply the Rank Hovis McDougall flour mill at Birkenhead Docks, where the severe curvature of the mill sidings precluded the use of bogie Grainflow Polybulks. RHM received approximately 15 Minibulks of wheat each week from Byford Grain at Chettisham, along with additional traffic from Newmarket, Royston or Whittlesford as required. BRT 7783 stands outside the mill at Birkenhead on 16 May 1985.

Right: In 1985 Standard Wagon built 22 bogie conflats, RLS 92610-31, for Pedigree Petfood. Leased from Railease, they initially carried 30ft curtain-sided containers from Melton Mowbray to Ardwick and Welwyn Garden City, but by 1994 these KFAs were on hire to Freightliner. RLS 92611 was awaiting unloading at Swindon in April 2000. The insulated containers carried Anchor Butter from New Zealand and had arrived as part of a dedicated weekly train from the OCL terminal at Tilbury.

Above: It was not until 1986 that private-owner stock regained a foothold in the domestic coal market, when Standard Wagon began building 172 two-axle conflats for Cawoods. CAWD 92703-874 had a low floor to accommodate containers up to 9ft high on approved routes and fit beneath the loading screens at the collieries and coal preparation plants. By 1988 up to 10 trains a week were running from various collieries, including Clipstone, Daw Mill and Lynemouth, and the washeries at Coedbach, Onllwyn and Wernos to Cawoods newly opened export berth at Ellesmere Port from where the containers were shipped to Ireland. There were also trains from the phurnacite plants at Abercwmboi and Immingham. In 1992 the shipping operation moved to Liverpool's Seaforth Docks, but by 1999, as the demand for domestic coal declined, workings had reduced to no more than two trains a week before ending altogether in 2004. At the height of the traffic CAWD 92818 is loaded at the Firegold phurnacite plant at Immingham in October 1990.

13. CONTAINERISED COAL

Below: By 2000 many of the containers carried RJB Mining livery with what little Irish traffic that remained now originating at either Gascoigne Wood or Welbeck Colliery. CAWD 92709 was one of 22 PFAs at Warrington *en route* from Welbeck to Seaforth on 20 February 2000.

Right: In 1996, 44 PFAs were sold to British Gypsum, and that same year another 60 were purchased by British Fuels Ltd for a new Anglo-Scottish coal working from Gascoigne Wood to coal depots at Aberdeen, Elgin and Mossend. Gradually these wagons would be reprefixed BFL, but CAWD 92836 retained its original identity at Warrington in July 1996.

Below: In 1987 Procor also built a batch of 41-tonne-glw low-deck two-axle conflats for containerised coal. PR 93201-40 were leased to Kellys, a Belfast-based company, with five trains a week running from either Abercwmboi, Coedbach or Onllwyn to Swansea Docks. In contrast to the Cawoods containers, which were loaded on board ship, the Kelly boxes were emptied into Dragon Shipping bulk carriers sailing from Swansea to Ireland and to mainland Europe. For several months two of the PFAs, PR 93209/40, could be seen on the West Highland line on trial with containers of fresh fish from Mallaig to Hull, but nothing came of the experiment, and by March 1988 they were back in South Wales. By August 1991 Kellys had ceased trading, and PR 93234 was in store at Swansea Burrows Sidings. In 1992 all 40 would be sold to the Ministry of Defence.

14. SCRAP METAL

Above and below: Steel scrap has long been an important business on rail, and in the 1980s three fleets of air-braked private-owner wagons were built to replace the ageing 16-ton minerals then used for this traffic. The largest fleet comprised 180 Railease two-axle 51-tonne-glw 34-tonne-capacity POAs, built with the aid of a £2.52 million Section 8 Grant in three batches at Heywood between 1982 and 1984 to feed the British Steel electric-arc furnaces at Aldwarke and Stocksbridge. More than 30 loading-points for this fleet have been identified, the majority in the Midlands and the North

East, but they could be found at scrapyards as far afield as Barrow and Brentford, and Silvertown and Swindon.

After the construction in 1978 of a demonstrator numbered RLS 5900 the first production batch of 20 followed in 1982, although RLS 5901-20 were built with extra bracing to the sides and ends. Large side doors were fitted for cleaning out any foreign material that might remain in the wagon once the steel scrap had been removed by an electro-magnet. Given the harsh environment in which these vehicles worked it was not uncommon to see them looking the worse for wear, as evidenced by RLS 5900, back at Heywood to be rebodied in May 1986, and RLS 5904, found in Warrington Arpley Yard on 18 May 1985 *en route* to Lowton Metals at Ashton-in-Makerfield.

Right: With experience gained from the first batch, the remaining POAs had an additional horizontal bracing rib while the door design was changed to a much smaller rectangular one situated on the centre line just above the solebar. RLS 5000-99 used underframes recovered from withdrawn BSC Ravenscraig Covhops, and RLS 5921-80 were built from scratch with Gloucester floating-axle suspension. However, soon after entering service it was found that small pieces of scrap such as turnings were collecting on the prominent ledges formed by the horizontal bracing which would then be blown off in transit causing danger and discomfort to permanent way staff and passengers waiting on station platforms. The remedy was to fit angled plates to the ledges to deflect spilled scrap onto the ground during loading, and both RLS 5049 and RLS 5966 had been so modified when recorded at Crossley Bros' scrapyard in Shipley in September 1985.

Above: Crossley's also loaded bogie opens for Sheerness Steel and on 4 October 1984 a Class 31 heads away from Shipley with the daily Speedlink to Leeds Hunslet Yard with two Procor PXAs on the first leg of their journey to Kent.

Right: The PXAs were from a batch of 40 built at Horbury Junction in 1982/3 using Schlieren bogies recovered from redundant tank wagons. PR 3100-39 were 102-tonne-glw, 73-tonne-capacity wagons, some 58ft over headstocks. They remained in Sheerness Steel traffic until 1995, when many were leased by European Metals Recycling to carry export scrap from Handsworth, Laisterdyke and Swindon to Liverpool Docks. Eventually they were repainted plain blue, but on 2 October 1997 PR 3103 retained its old livery when seen at Swindon. Indeed, it still carried its original POA TOPS code, which had not been amended to PXA, let alone JXA.

Left: In 1995, 15 of these bogie opens were leased by British Steel to operate between the galvanising works at Shotton and Port Talbot steelworks. Once again problems were encountered in transit, and the wagons were fitted with three-piece roof sections fabricated from old tank barrels. PR 3126 had just been modified when photographed at Stoke in October 1995.

Right: Scrap to the Allied Steel & Wire (AS&W) works in Cardiff continued to arrive in BR wagons until 1987, when Standard Wagon constructed forty 51-tonne-glw POAs on redundant PEA underframes. These were followed in 1989 by two batches of 46-tonners — RLS 4585-606/8 from Standard, built on unwanted PMA and PRA chassis, and PDUF 4500-59/80-84 from Powell Duffryn, utilising old Shell TTA and APCM PCA underframes. All were painted black, and the fleet became known as the 'Black Adders', the nickname deriving from the title of a popular television series. Until the reopening of the Trafford Park Estate railway Ardwick Goods was used as a loading-point, and a grubby RLS 5215 was one of three POAs in the yard on 15 February 1988.

Left: The Standard-built 46-tonners were adorned with a large yellow diamond to help staff distinguish them quickly from their larger cousins and were regular visitors to Norton's scrapyard in Trafford Park. RLS 4595 waits loading in November 1989.

Above: Second-hand underframes, this time from ex-Clyde Cement bogie PDAs RLS 9800-35, were used for the next batch of scrap opens for AS&W, which gradually replaced the earlier two-axle fleet on workings to Cardiff. Recently converted TIPH 9806, coded JNA, awaits clearance to enter traffic at Stoke on 15 June 1997.

Below: As well as the more-established traffics there were also other workings such as the movement of baled scrap from Ashton Road to Lackenby, and from Shotton to Ravenscraig. Tiger Rail 46-tonne opens, no longer required for aggregate traffic, were often allocated to such flows and TRL 5413 was recorded at Ardwick Goods in April 1989 waiting to be shunted into the neighbouring carriage & wagon works at Ashton Road.

Left and below left: In addition to scrap from Shotton, Ravenscraig received a limited amount of its local supply by rail, and in 1989 D. Christie of Camlachie purchased from BR 29 MDV 21-tonne minerals wagons, which were duly renumbered as CHR 4609-37. However, their use from Camlachie seems to have been short-lived, for by March 1990 20 had already been relegated to internal use at Ravenscraig and the other nine, now repainted and lettered 'MC', were working from MC Processors at St Rollox. CHR 4625 (formerly B312498) and CHR 4635 (ex B313486) were photographed at Ravenscraig No 1 Yard and St Rollox respectively in July 1990. *Author, courtesy Trevor Mann*

Above, left and bottom: In 1999 Marcroft fitted seven PFA conflats with Translift turntables to enable the transhipment of waste skips between road and rail without the need for any facilities other than road access. The concept was aimed at the recycling business, for the transfer point would not need a special licence, as the containers never touched the ground. In 2000, BRT 92603-9 began carrying skips of scrap aluminium (shredded aluminium cans and aluminium furnace dross) from a transfer siding at Arpley Down Sidings, Warrington, to Burrows Sidings, Swansea, from where the skips were transported by road to a recycling plant at Gowerton. Empty BRT 92605 and loaded BRT 92607 were noted at Warrington on 16 April 2000. Most skips were sheeted, but on 24 September 2000 BRT 92605 was seen again, this time loaded with a skip fitted with a telescopic cover. By 2004 the aluminium traffic had ended, but the PFAs remained on hire to European Metals Recycling, carrying skips of steel scrap from Plymouth Cattewater to Cardiff Docks.

15. RADIOACTIVE WASTE

Left: Since 1983 British Nuclear Fuels Ltd has operated a mixed fleet of wagons to carry low-level radioactive waste, such as contaminated clothing and tools, from the nuclear reprocessing facility at Sellafield to a disposal site at Drigg four miles away down the Cumbrian coast. At first 30 modified ex-BR OBA wagons, renumbered BNFL 91000-29, were used to carry the waste in covered skips, but in the 1990s these were transferred to work as barrier wagons in nuclear-flask trains. They were replaced on the Drigg service by three bogie and 23 two-axle conflats. BNFL 91002 was at Warrington in October 1993 accompanying a bogie flask wagon *en route* to Shirebrook for overhaul.

Left: BNFL's three KFAs, BNFL 95474/5/84, were purchased from Railease in 1994, having been built at Heywood in 1983 as part of a 17-strong batch of 56ft conflats designed to carry containers of potash from Boulby to Severnside. Repainted and re-prefixed BNFL 95475 was seen shortly after leaving Sellafield for Drigg early on a frosty 9 March 2005.

Below: Apart from BNFL 95050, purpose-built at Heywood in 1991, the other 22 two-axle conflats were acquired second-hand from Cawoods. Reprefixed DRSL (for Direct Rail Services — the company established by BNFL in 1996), they have also been used to carry special nuclear flasks between Barrow Docks and Sellafield as well as containers of contaminated steel scrap from Workington Docks to Drigg. Various designs of containers have been carried, including these odd-looking boxes loaded on two of the ex-Cawoods PFAs, DRSL 92766/17, seen returning to Sellafield from Drigg in March 2005.

16. CAR-CARRIERS

Above: As car ownership grew in the 1960s the delivery of new cars became big business for BR, and in 1963 distribution company MAT Transauto introduced more than 150 Carflats converted from ex-Southern Railway coach underframes by South Staffs Wagon at Tipton. Numbered in the range MAT 94000-153, they had by 1980 been replaced on most flows by purpose-built double-deck wagons, but around 30 'flats, all fitted with air brakes, were retained to convey high-sided commercial and utility vehicles. They had a wooden deck, low fixed framework sides and full-width drop ends, loose-spiked chocks being used to secure the load. Recorded at Dover on 6 October 1988, MAT 94022 was one of two PFBs, each loaded with four Range Rovers, that had just arrived from Bordesley. Initially these wagons had been allocated ferry diagram E.033, but by this date they no longer went abroad, and they were about to be shunted to the MAT compound at Dover Military Siding, from where the cars would be driven onto a ferry.

Above: Unlike Rover, Vauxhall made only limited use of rail, but in the 1980s new vehicles for customers in Scotland and Northern Ireland were brought by road from the company's factory at Ellesmere Port to the old Motorail sidings at Newton-le-Willows, where MAT had opened a small depot. The bulk of the rail traffic comprised cars destined for Leith or Stranraer Harbour, but in March 1987 MAT 94136 was found behind the station platform, loaded with commercial vehicles for Exeter St Davids.

Above: The double-deck Cartic 4 sets were articulated on five bogies to save weight and ran on small, 2ft 8in-diameter wheels to fit within the loading gauge. MAT bought 100 sets: 23 from Rootes Pressings in 1966, 17 from Standard Wagon in 1970 and 60 from BREL Ashford in 1971. All had a maximum speed of 75mph and each set could accommodate up to 34 cars. Over the years they saw use in numerous workings including Chryslers from Linwood to Gosford Green and Windsor Bridge, Manchester; Fords from Halewood to Elderslie, and imported Citroëns and Peugeots from Queenborough to Bathgate and Leith. They could also be found handling short-term traffics such as Skodas from Harwich to King's Lynn and Mazdas from Queenborough to Selby, but by 1991 their main task was moving Rover cars from Cowley and Longbridge to Dover, Purfleet and Southampton for export.

The allocation of individual TOPS numbers to each element of a Cartic 4 set was unusual, given that they could only operate as a unit and so the MAT fleet became MAT 90000-399. Set 493 (MAT 90356-9) occupied one of the two sidings at Newton-le-Willows in July 1985. Set numbers 424-6 were never used, while set 427 comprised MAT 90092-6.

Centre left and left: In 1986 MAT began fitting plastic side screens to its PJAs to combat increased vandalism. MAT 90216 from set 458, was at Cowley in September 1991 with Minis for Southampton, while MAT 90085, part of set 422, had a similar load in April 1995.

Above: The 25 Railease Carflats RLS 94400-24, converted from BR Mk 1 coaches in 1979, were also used on a variety of automotive traffic, including Renaults from Goole to Perth, Vauxhalls from Luton to Bathgate and Ford Transits from Eastleigh to Garston. Recently repainted RLS 94410 heads north from Eastleigh on 14 September 1989.

Below: Ten years later the Ford traffic was in the hands of various internationally registered single-deck car-carriers plus the three STVA Lowtic sets converted at Stoke in 1998 from MAT Cartics. STVA 90012-5 had been detached at Didcot with binding brakes on 25 May 1999.

17. WEEDKILLERS AND WATER CANNONS

Left: Controlling the spread of weeds on the railway is vital for the safe running of trains, for vegetation can quickly destabilise ballast and impair the sighting of signals. For many years Chipman Chemicals and Fisons operated specially equipped spraying trains which visited every corner of the national network at least once a year.

It will come as no surprise that many of the vehicles owned by Chipman, based in Horsham, West Sussex, were ex-Southern Railway stock, and in addition to several modified Maunsell and Bulleid coaches it used two former Scenery vans. Spray van CC 99014 (previously S4600S) and staff van CC 99015 (S4589S) were photographed at Watford in October 1985 together with four 35-ton tanks (purchased in 1977 from Esso) which Chipman used to carry water.

Right: In 1985 the Chipman contract also covered the Western Region, and on 7 June CC 99014 was photographed in action near Quainton, on the single-track line between Aylesbury and Claydon Junction.

Below: In 1992 CC 99014 was fitted with high-pressure water jets to assist in the annual battle against leaf mulch, which if left unchecked collects on the railhead and compromises train adhesion and braking. By June 1999, however, it had been withdrawn and was awaiting disposal at Horsham.

Left: Water-cannon duties were taken over by three former Motorail vans purchased by Nomix-Chipman in 1997, and that October two of the vans, CC 99026 and CC 99027 (ex 96104 and 96154), were to be found at Neville Hill TMD in Leeds.

Right and below: Operating with the two KCAs were four 45-ton tanks hired from E. G. Steele. Built by Metro-Cammell in 1966, STL 54855/9/60/8 had been part of a 15-strong batch of TTAs owned by Texaco and used to carry Class A petroleum products from Avonmouth to Exeter City Basin. Sold to W. H. Davis in 1980, 14 were acquired by Steele in 1984, when two were leased to Harris Bros to carry molasses from Greenock to Inverurie, while the rest went into methanol traffic from ICI Haverton Hill. Now a water tank, freshly painted STL 54868 waits for its next tour of duty at Neville Hill on 12 October 1997.

Each water-cannon train consisted of a spray van and two water tanks top-and-tailed by a pair of Class 37 locomotives, the vehicles being connected by several pipes and hoses. The vans, which were also used to apply Sandite to the railhead to improve adhesion, were transferred to Railtrack in 1998, becoming LNE 99025-7.

Above and below: Nomix-Chipman also owned a drain-cleaning train constructed by RFS at Doncaster in 1992 on two former Freightliner flats. CC 95490 (formerly 601764), equipped with a sludge tank and a power supply, and CC 95491 (ex 601797), with two water tanks and mess accommodation, are seen at Reading, the train's home base, in March 1993.

As the train moved along a section of track water was blasted down a hose into the drain to dislodge any accumulation of leaves, litter or other debris, and the remaining liquid was then sucked back into the sludge tank for disposal subsequently. In 1998 the 'drain train' was sold to Railtrack, the wagons being re-prefixed 'SRL' and rebranded 'Sussex Rail'.

18. CHEMICALS FROM IMMINGHAM

Right: Developed by the Great Central Railway, the port of Immingham is an important centre for coal, iron ore, petroleum and chemicals, and from 1990 styrene monomer, the polymer for polystyrene (a plastic familiar to railway modellers) was transported by rail from Immingham to the Atochem factory at Stalybridge. Eleven former Class B bogie tank wagons — BRT 84090-4/9, built in 1968 by R. Y. Pickering for Gulf, and PR 82602-6, built in 1969 by Standard Wagon for Chevron — were converted at Horbury for this working, which ran twice a week as a 10-wagon set (leaving one vehicle spare), and between 1993 and 1999 the wagons were also used to carry styrene monomer to Stalybridge from the BP Chemicals works at Baglan Bay. The conversion entailed removal of the tanks' insulation and outer cladding and through vacuum pipes, replacement of the manlids and discharge valves, and a repaint into a blue livery. BRT 84099, now coded TEA, was spare at Immingham in September 1990.

Centre right: The styrene monomer was loaded at the Immingham Dock Tank Farm, to the north of the inner dock. Other rail traffic handled at this terminal included caustic soda, methanol and white spirit, and on 1 August 1990 both styrene for Stalybridge and methanol for Lindsey refinery were being loaded.

Below: To meet increased demand at Stalybridge three more former petroleum tanks (PR 82613/26 and BRT 84133) were added to the pool in 1999, before all 14 second-hand wagons were replaced by a new build in 2001. Constructed by Marcroft at Stoke, CAIB 88081-93 carried an impressive 76 tonnes — 5 tonnes more than the earlier tanks. CAIB 88083 was captured at Immingham in May 2004. *courtesy Mark Saunders*

Above and below: Sodium hydroxide, commonly known as caustic soda, is one of the most widely used chemicals in industry and as home production began to decline in the 1980s imported traffic became increasingly significant. Caustic soda was forwarded from Immingham on behalf of Atochem and Dow Chemicals to the Roche pharmaceutical plant at Dalry, British Sidac's cellulose works at Wigton, and Albright & Wilson at Corkickle. Both Atochem and Dow leased 46- and 51-tonne tanks from Procor and Tiger Rail, those operated by Atochem having previously worked for ICI. TRL 51636, photographed at Immingham in March 1988, was the only TTA seen with the large logo; others, such as PR 58743 seen here, which came from a batch of 120 tanks built for ICI by Standard Wagon in 1968, had to make do with a plain 'ATO' in place of the ICI roundel.

Above: Also recorded at Immingham in September 1990 was PR 58506, one of eight TTBs hired by Dow that retained their original suspension. Built by Standard in 1971, they came from a batch of 105 lagged caustic soda tanks that had previously been leased to BP Chemicals at Baglan Bay.

Below: Immingham was also the origin of a regular wagonload working of imported acrylonitrile, which was loaded at the acid plant on the eastern side of the docks and transported by rail to BP Chemicals at Barry for use in the production of nitrile rubber. In 1986 five Class A tanks (BPO 37273-7) fitted with buffer-override protection were allocated to this traffic, BPO 37277 (previously BPO 60568) being seen in Immingham yard that November.

19. INDUSTRIAL ACIDS

Left: Nitric acid is a component of many explosives, and during World War 2 the Ministry of Supply purchased a fleet of unfitted 14-ton tanks from several builders to supply munitions factories around the country. By the 1970s most of these wagons were restricted to internal use, but a handful remained in main-line traffic into the early 1980s, working between the Royal Ordnance Factory at Bishopton, near Glasgow, and the Nobel Explosives works at Ardeer, some 25 miles away on the Ayrshire coast.
MODA 40279, built by Charles Roberts in 1941 and coded TRO in 1974, was still in remarkably good condition when photographed at Bishopton in July 1990. The painting of abbreviated white and red warning bands only on the lower hemisphere of the barrel had been adopted in wartime so that tank wagons carrying hazardous loads could not be easily identified from above by enemy aircraft.

Left: A short distance down the line at one of the tank-filling stations located on the site at ROF Bishopton were three more 14-tonners, including MODA 40276. Unlike MODA 40279, on which the Hazchem label had the UN number '2031' for nitric acid, these three were labelled '1796', indicating 'acid mixtures or nitrating acid' — a sulphuric/nitric-acid mix used in the production of dynamite.

Right: Also at Bishopton in July 1990 were two modern air-braked 35-tonne-capacity monobloc tanks, MODA 56950/1, that had been built by Powell Duffryn in 1976 specifically to carry nitric acid to the Royal Ordnance factory at Highbridge (officially ROF Bridgwater). Having Gloucester pedestal suspension enabled them to run at 60mph in Speedlink trains between Scotland and Somerset, but this movement had ended by 1989, following which, filled with water, they were used as barrier wagons on special MoD trains running between Grangemouth Dock and Bishopton.

Right: The nuclear industry was another user of nitric acid, and the United Kingdom Atomic Energy Authority owned more than 50 tanks that were used to supply the Windscale reprocessing plant at Sellafield and the reactor-fuel-rod works at Salwick, near Preston. Inherited in the 1970s by British Nuclear Fuels Ltd, these tanks formed a Thursdays-only conditional block working booked to run from Bishopton to either Salwick or Sellafield as required. Built by Charles Roberts in 1950, BNFL 40600/7, coded TRO, were later preserved by the Lakeside & Haverthwaite Railway, and on a wet day in May 1992 the author was given special permission to venture along the track outside Haverthwaite station to photograph them.

Below: In 1982 UKF Fertilisers took over the contract to supply BNFL, the plan being to employ a fleet of 10 bogie acid tanks built by Charles Roberts in 1972 for use by UKF on inter-works traffic between Ince & Elton and Thames Haven. However, it was soon discovered that, despite their relatively short bogie-centre distance of 26ft 2in, BRT 84183-92 were unable to reach the unloading siding at Salwick, so six 'new' tanks, numbered TRL 51948-53, were built by Procor using components recovered from redundant glycol, chlorine and hydrocyanic-acid tank wagons. Together with loaded fertiliser vans, the nitric-acid tanks were tripped from Ince & Elton to Warrington, where the bogie tanks for Sellafield would be attached to the overnight Speedlink for the Cumbrian coast while the 'Baby Nitrics' went forward on a separate trip serving Burn Naze and Salwick. 'Baby Nitric' TRL 51948, built with the barrel from glycol tank TRL 51224 and the air-braked underframe from HCN tank TRL 51440, stands in Warrington Walton Old Junction Yard *en route* to Salwick on 9 September 1990.

Left: In 1991 the BNFL Ince & Elton–Salwick workings, generally comprising two tanks per week, ceased, although the Sellafield traffic survived the closure of the Speedlink network, running as a Saturdays-only out-and-back diagram. The train was slip-worked at Sellafield, the previous week's wagons, now discharged, being due back at Ince & Elton by late afternoon. However, weekend engineering on 10 September 1994 disrupted this schedule, and the discharged tanks, including BRT 84190, were stabled in Warrington Arpley. By this date only five bogie nitrics were still in use, all having been repainted the previous year in Kemira livery.

Right and below right: In 1970 Leathers Chemicals opened a sulphuric-acid plant at St Helens. Initial rail traffic included the movement of over 25,000 tons a year to Monsanto's acrylonitrile works at Seal Sands, on Teesside, in a weekly block train of up to eight bogie tanks, but this company train ceased to run in 1983, when Monsanto began making greater use of imported acid. Although there were still occasional wagonloads despatched to Teesside, the bulk of the sulphuric acid from St Helens thereafter went to the Roche plant at Dalry for use as a catalyst in the manufacture of ascorbic acid (Vitamin C).

Built in France by CFPM and leased from E. G. Steele, STL 85703-10 were 102-tonne-glw TEAs of 78-tonne capacity, their small barrels being a characteristic of sulphuric acid tanks, given the high specific gravity of the acid. After Leathers was bought by Hays Chemicals in 1985 the tanks were repainted, and STL 85703 was recorded thus at Warrington Walton Old Junction in October 1988. The first wagon allocated the number STL 85709 was wrecked in a derailment at Beattock in 1973, ironically when returning from repair at Hamilton, and Standard Wagon built a replacement in 1976. Fitted with full-length solebars and lacking the company lettering, the new STL 85709 was easy to identify and is seen here at Warrington Bank Quay with another load for Dalry in September 1985. Internationally registered ferry tanks later took over this working, and STL 85709 was the last of the batch to remain in traffic, finally being withdrawn in 1995.

Above: Sulphuric acid was also produced by the Imperial Smelting Corporation at Avonmouth, as a by-product in the processing of zinc sulphide. ISC owned and leased a variety of tank wagons, the last batch being 17 former chlorine tanks modified by Procor in 1983 to carry acid. Regular recipients supplied from Avonmouth included Gower Chemicals at Swansea, Berk Spencer Acids at Stratford Market and the Royal Ordnance factory at Highbridge; after these flows ended in 1991 the TTAs were used to carry sulphuric acid from Seal Sands to British Sidac at Wigton. TRL 51109 is seen at Port Clarence in May 1993.

Below: Hydrochloric acid is obtained as a by-product in the electrolysis of salt and in the manufacture of chlorinated hydrocarbons, but although large quantities are produced there is little resultant rail traffic, as most of the acid is used in 'down-stream' processes on-site. However, until 1986 there was an inter-works flow from the chlorobenzene plant at ICI's Hillhouse Works at Burn Naze to Runcorn, carried in a small batch of TTBs built in 1966 by Standard Wagon. PR 58219 was one of six hydrochloric-acid tanks found in store at Burn Naze during a works visit in 1987.

Above: Between 2001 and 2006 there was a regular weekly working of two or three tanks of hydrochloric acid from the Albion Inorganics works at Sandbach to Dalry. This flow resulted from a modification to the production processes at Dalry and replaced inbound salt traffic, which had been a feature of Roche's rail operations for many years. For the new order W. H. Davis converted seven ex-Shell Class B TEAs, which were renumbered as WHD 83901-7. The former SUKO 83751, renumbered WHD 83906, was photographed at Warrington in August 2003.

Below: Phosphoric acid, also known as orthophosphoric acid, is used in compound fertilisers and in the manufacture of detergents. In 1968 Fisons Fertiliser leased 24 air-braked two-axle phosphoric-acid tanks from Standard Wagon for a twice-weekly block train working from its works at Avonmouth and Immingham to the recently opened Shellstar (later UKF Fertiliser) plant at Ince & Elton. PA/1, the first of the fleet, was photographed at Heywood in 1968. By 1975 they had been fitted with pedestal suspension, while TOPS saw PA/1-9 renumbered PR 58901-9, PA/10-24 becoming PR 58410-24.

Above: Following the takeover in 1983 of Fisons Fertiliser by Norsk Hydro, UKF obtained its phosphoric acid from Albright & Wilson at Corkickle, and before the new working commenced these tanks were rebuilt with twin fillers and buffer over-rides. They were also repainted in UKF livery, as demonstrated by PR 58906 at Ince & Elton in November 1984.

Below: The Marchon works at Corkickle was also the loading-point for Albright & Wilson's own fleet of 22 phosphoric-acid tanks, built by Standard Wagon in 1972. Fitted from new with pedestal suspension, they were built to supply the Associated Chemical Co fertiliser works at Barton-on-Humber, near Immingham, ACC being another Albright & Wilson subsidiary. A weekly block train of up to 20 TUBs ran until the works at Barton closed in 1986. As 51-tonners with air brakes and a through vacuum pipe PR 70000-21 should have been stencilled 'TUB', but PR 70013 was still incorrectly coded 'TTF' when found in store at Healey Mills in November 1988.

20. CYCLOHEXANE TANKS

Left: In 1969 Charles Roberts built 36 air-braked 30-tonne capacity two-axle tank wagons to carry cyclohexane feedstock from the ICI petrochemical complex at Wilton, Teesside, to the company's new nylon factory at Ardeer. Twelve more tanks were built in 1971, and in 1978 a further six were constructed by Standard Wagon to a modified design. However, worldwide over-production of nylon led to the closure of the Ayrshire plant in 1980, rendering the wagons redundant.

The traffic had been conveyed in a block train of up to 20 wagons two or three times a week, but it went largely unheeded by the railway-enthusiast fraternity. Indeed, the only photograph the author has seen of the working appeared in *BR Freight Services In Focus* (Ian Allan 1982), albeit mistakenly identified as an oil train. Fifteen tanks were subsequently employed on methanol traffic from ICI's Billingham Works, but by 1986 the entire fleet was out of use. Many of the original design, numbered TRL 51895-930/6-47 on TOPS, ended their days at Connah's Quay, where lack of space saw them stored at right angles to the track. TRL 51938, built 1971 and coded TTB, sits on the ground in May 1991.

Below: Photographed in store at Wilton in March 1988, TRL 55523 came from the final batch of cyclohexane tanks built as TTAs to an updated design in 1978 with pedestal suspension. TRL 55520-5 had a working life of less than 18 months, which must be something of a record. *courtesy Trevor Mann*

Right: The Associated Octel Co Ltd manufactured 'anti-knock compound', a mixture of tetra-ethyl lead (TEL) and ethylene dibromide which in the 1920s had been discovered to increase the octane levels of aviation and motor spirits and hence improve engine performance. From its opening in 1954 Octel's main works at Ellesmere Port became the base for a varied fleet of chemical-tank wagons.

The company forwarded considerable traffic to the Continent via the train ferries, and this will be considered in a future volume covering ferry wagons, but there were also regular workings of chlorine from Ellesmere Port to the bromine plants at Amlwch and Hayle. In 1957 Hurst Nelson built 35 unfitted 14-ton chlorine tanks, 34 of which survived to become AO 47009-42 on TOPS. Hayle closed in 1973, but the TROs remained in traffic to Amlwch, being air-piped and recoded 'TRQ' in 1977. After withdrawal in 1982, AO 47023/42 were preserved on what is now the Embsay & Bolton Abbey Steam Railway.

21. ASSOCIATED OCTEL

Below: Nineteen 27-ton-capacity ferry-fitted chlorine tanks, built by Charles Roberts in four batches between 1967 and 1977, were also used on these workings, although in 1981 their international registration was cancelled, and they were renumbered AO 55339-57. Like all chlorine-tank wagons they were painted in the mandatory livery for liquid gas tanks, which, from 1968, required a white barrel with a 300mm-wide yellow band around the midriff; commodity warning plates, painted yellow with black lettering, were also fixed on top of each solebar. This livery persists today, although by the 1980s the yellow band had become orange in colour.

On 8 September 1991 AO 55341 was awaiting repairs at Marcroft Engineering's outstation just outside the Octel works at Ellesmere Port. The wagon's international origins are evident from the presence of yellow chaining-down rings and cleats on the underframe as well as from the brake platform at the far end, which housed the handbrake stanchion; apparently it was considered that the platform railings provided sufficient protection, as buffer-override beams were not fitted at that end.

Left: To replace the TRQs Octel leased 15 air-braked 46-tonne-glw chlorine tanks from Tiger Rail, and after gaining the characteristic octagonal company logo TRL 51562-5/7-77 worked between Ellesmere Port and Amlwch until the traffic ended in 1993. TRL 51564 was photographed at Ellesmere Port in August 1992. Built by Charles Roberts in 1966 as one of 25 TTBs initially owned by Tank Rentals Ltd and leased to ICI, it had been upgraded with buffer over-rides but retained its original UIC double-link suspension and 13-plate leaf springs.

Below left: The Associated Octel works at Amlwch and Hayle used chlorine to extract bromine from seawater, much of the bromine then being converted into ethylene dibromide and transported by rail back to Ellesmere Port. By the late 1960s there was also a requirement to transport ethylene dibromide to Octel's affiliated works on the Continent, and in 1970 Charles Roberts built a batch of 46-ton ferry tanks for this purpose. However, in common with the chlorine tanks they were not accepted by all overseas administrations, and in 1981 they were renumbered AO 55325-38 and confined to the Amlwch–Ellesmere Port circuit. AO 55334 is seen in Ellesmere Port East Sidings on 20 September 1992.

Above right: A handful of chlorine and anti-knock tanks had been converted to handle ethylene dibromide, and when they were withdrawn in 1982 Standard Wagon built six replacements using second-hand barrels and new Gloucester pedestal-suspension underframes. Numbered AO 55319-24, they were, like the rest of the Associated Octel fleet, kept in immaculate condition, AO 55322 being seen thus outside the works at Ellesmere Port on 14 April 1991.

Above right: With approximately 50% of the company's rail shipments being destined for the Continent it made sense that all Octel's 'anti-knock' tank wagons should be ferry-fitted, as they could also be used to supply refineries in Britain. In addition to the workings from Ellesmere Port there was also wagonload traffic from Octel's smaller works at Plumley, near Northwich. Plumley had been Britain's first anti-knock factory, opened by the British Ethyl Corporation in 1940 with financial backing from the Air Ministry to ensure a supply of TEL for the Royal Air Force. In 1961 it was converted to produce tetra-methyl lead (TML), a more volatile compound better suited to high-performance engines (being used alone or blended with TEL), which led to a regular inter-works move of six or seven tanks a week between Plumley and Ellesmere Port.

By the 1970s most of the early 35-ton-glw anti-knock tanks dating from 1954 had been replaced in ferry service by larger vehicles, and 24 were renumbered in the range AO 48462-91 for use solely in Britain. Each carrying 19½ tons, these insulated anchor-mounted tanks were a common

sight on the aforementioned inter-works traffic, AO 48470 being one of three TSRs photographed at Ellesmere Port loaded with TML from Plumley on 27 April 1985. The 'double C' marking above the TML sticker indicated that the wagon was covered by the 'Commuted Charges' scheme with regard to shunting and siding rental.

Later in 1985, following the closure of Plumley, most of the TSRs were withdrawn, but AO 48483-91, which had already been fitted with air brakes, were retained until 1991 to supply the refineries at Grangemouth and Robeston. Both anti-knock compound and ethylene dibromide are highly poisonous, and the tanks were required to be painted either aluminium or grey, with detailed warning boards, explaining the hazard, fixed to the solebar. Furthermore, like the chlorine and ethylene-dibromide tanks these vehicles were designed to be loaded and unloaded from the top only, a lockable 'bonnet' cover being fitted over the valves on top of the barrel to protect them from damage in the event of an accident or fire.

22. VAN DEN BERGH & JURGENS

Above and below: In May 1986 a new service commenced between Purfleet and Bromborough, near Port Sunlight, conveying hot edible oil on behalf of margarine producer Van den Bergh & Jurgens. Twenty-four bogie Class B petroleum-tank wagons were purchased from Shell and, after being refurbished (by Crump, at Connah's Quay) with new insulation, cladding and heating tubes, were renumbered VDBJ 82500-23.

Carrying 730 tons of edible oil, the trains ran four days a week, two sets of 10 wagons being in use and four wagons held as spares at Purfleet. However, by 1991 two tanks had already been withdrawn after suffering a barrel implosion during unloading, and in 1992 the traffic was discontinued, the tanks being purchased by CAIB and subsequently leased to Total for transporting fuel oil and bitumen from Lindsey.

A visit to Connah's Quay in March 1986 found a pristine VDBJ 82501 (ex-SUKO 83124) waiting to enter service, while VDBJ 82521 (ex-SUKO 83101) was noted at Ellesmere Port Sidings in August 1992 *en route* to Jake Rail Tank Cleaning Services for washing-out.

23. JAKE RTCS

Below: Jake Rail Tank Cleaning Services (TOPS location 38321) was located just west of Ellesmere Port station, next to the line to Hooton, on the site of the old Shropshire Union Railway & Canal Co's locomotive depot. In 1922 the shed had been taken over by the Manchester Ship Canal Co, but after the latter moved to a new depot near to the town's docks in 1972 the old building was demolished, Jake's opening on the vacant site in 1979.

As its title suggested, the company's main activity at the works was tank-wagon cleaning, both external and internal, and in the 1980s around 20 two-axle tanks (or the equivalent in bogie tanks) were being cleaned per week, the majority coming from Shell's Stanlow refinery, which was

less than three miles away. In the 1990s Jake's took on more repainting work and also began servicing other wagon types such as cement PCAs and petroleum coke hoppers, but oil-tank wagons remained the mainstay of the business until it closed in 2002.

Rail access was via a spur off the Manchester Ship Canal line at Ellesmere Port West Junction, and immediately inside the gate the single track split into four short sidings, none more than 216ft in length. This view from the rail entrance showing the entire site was recorded on the occasion of the author's last visit, in July 2002, by which date rail traffic had all but ceased. On the left, with its curved roof, is the paint shop, with accommodation on its two tracks for two bogie or four two-axle tanks, while the smaller building to the right, next to the main line, contained the shot-blasting booth, which could accommodate one bogie or two two-axle wagons at a time.

Right: A line of EWS CSA powder wagons stand in the overgrown loop outside Jake's works in July 2002. In busier times the trackwork in this area had been well maintained.

Above: The Manchester Ship Canal Co would shunt Jake's yard shortly after breakfast, and on 15 January 1991 the author recorded MSC 3004, one of the company's 325hp 0-6-0DH Rolls-Royce 'Sentinels', in the loop. It had just hauled the two repainted Shell tanks out of Jake's and after having run round would propel them into one of the otherwise disused sidings at Ellesmere Port West for collection by BR later in the day.

Below: Jake's own industrial locomotive, four-wheel, chain-driven Ruston & Hornsby No 466626, an '88DS' type that had previously belonged to Bowater, poses with SUKO 67046 outside the paint shop on 16 January 1994.

PRIVATE-OWNER WAGONS IN COLOUR

Right: The time taken to clean a wagon, both inside and out, would vary depending on the state of the vehicle, but it was rare for a wagon to remain at Jake's for more than a week. As space was at a premium much of the cleaning was undertaken outdoors, and on 27 September 1994 two young employees were busy washing down SUKO 68021. The SUKO 68000-59 batch of TTAs had all previously been unlagged Class B tanks numbered in the SUKO 655xx, 656xx and 657xx series (SUKO 68021 having been SUKO 65600), renumbering being effected in 1992 after conversion to carry Class A products.

Below: Esso tanks, used for carrying Class A, bitumen and liquid petroleum gas, also made regular appearances at Jake's prior to going on to Crewe Works for general repair, and on 17 September 1994 ESSO 56131, together with ESSO 56121, was to be found in Ellesmere Port East Sidings. By this date all surviving Esso Class A tanks had been re-sprung and concentrated at Fawley for traction-gas-oil traffic.

24. TRACTION GAS OIL AND LUBRICATING OIL

Destination	M	T	W	Th	F
Allerton TMD	-	-	2	-	2
Barrow-in-Furness FP	1	-	-	-	-
Birkenhead Mollington Street TMD	1	-	-	-	-
Buxton TMD	-	-	1	-	1
Chester TMD	1	-	-	1	1
Crewe Diesel TMD	4	-	4	-	-
Holyhead SD	-	-	1	-	1
Llandudno Junction SD	1	-	-	-	-
Manchester Longsight TMD	-	3	-	2	-
Manchester Newton Heath TMD	-	4	-	3	-
Machynlleth FP	-	1	-	-	-
Toton TMD	2	-	2	-	1
Wigan Springs Branch TMD	-	-	2	-	2

TMD   Traction Maintenance Depot
FP   Fuelling Point
SD   Stabling Depot

Above: Diesel-locomotive fuel ('traction gas oil' in railway parlance) has been a significant source of traffic since the 1960s, and as few depots had any significant storage capacity (or the space to store large numbers of wagons) they received a few tanks every day or so. Most were served from their nearest refinery, and until March 1998 the Shell refinery at Stanlow in Cheshire supplied locomotive depots and fuelling points in North Wales and North West England. By way of example, the accompanying table records the number of tank wagons (all SUKO 45-ton-glw TTA or TTB) despatched from Stanlow loaded with TGO in the week commencing Monday 23 January 1984.

While not a Class A petroleum product (*i.e.* one with a flash point below 21°C), traction-gas oil was often transported in spare Class A tank wagons such as SUKO 67247. Pictured in the BR yard at Trafford Park on 15 September 1990, it was one of three TTAs waiting to be tripped across Manchester to Longsight TMD. It was built by Powell Duffryn of Cardiff in 1967 and by the date of this photograph, in common with the majority of the Shell fleet, had been fitted with parabolic springs.

Traction-gas oil was forwarded in wagonload freight services until the demise of Speedlink in 1991, when the Petroleum sector was forced to introduce its own dedicated workings.

Above and right: Class B tanks (for products with a flash point of 21°C or above) such as SUKO 65652, photographed at Ellesmere Port on 21 April 1990, were more commonly seen in traction-gas-oil traffic. Shell began adding the red and yellow striping to its Class A and unlagged Class B tanks in 1989, but the age-old problem of keeping wagons clean eventually led to a change of heart, and from 1995 these were removed. However, the outline of the Shell logo and the stripes would often remain evident, as on SUKO 65634, recorded at Wigan Springs Branch TMD on 1 June 1996. Both these Class B tanks had been built by Powell Duffryn in 1966.

Right: When traffic from Esso's pipeline-fed terminal at Colwick ceased in 1988 Total and Petrofina, joint owners of the Lindsey oil refinery at Immingham, took over the contract to supply the Eastern Region's locomotive depots and fuelling points. For this, 51 ex-BRTE and Procor two-axle 46-tonne tanks were refurbished for Total and renumbered in the series PR 58230-80. PR 58254 (previously BRT 57456) was recorded at the otherwise deserted stabling sidings outside Cleethorpes station one morning in May 1991.

Left: As well as operating its own TTAs Fina also leased six 51-tonners from Tiger Rail, and TRL 70728-33, built by Procor for Esso in 1977, were a common sight in Immingham yard. TRL 70733, loaded with TGO for Thornaby TMD, waits to leave on 8 September 1990.

Right: Many locomotive depots would also receive the occasional tank of lubricating oil by rail, and in the 1980s such workings from Stanlow were handled by a batch of 12 former Class B tanks renumbered SUKO 65900-11. After 1988 these wagons were no longer loaded within the main refinery but at the GATX tank farm located at the end of the Manchester Ship Canal Co's Eastham branch, to the west of Ellesmere Port. MSC records reveal that in 1989 some 149 separate tank loads of lubricating oil were despatched by rail from Eastham to 34 TMDs throughout the country. SUKO 65900 (ex SUKO 63900), built by Pickering in 1967, waits alongside the loading racks inside GATX on 23 January 1991.

Left: As there were no mandatory livery requirements applicable to wagons engaged in such traffic when British Petroleum began moving lubricating oil between its refineries at Llandarcy and Grangemouth, the five TTAs allocated to the working (BPO 60194, 67191, 67774, 67787 and 67885) were repainted into a special scheme to ensure that they would not be loaded with another product by mistake. BPO 60194, built by Charles Roberts in 1964, was photographed at Railcar Services, Stoke, on a wet afternoon in August 1986. Note the inaccurate TOPS code (TTF), despite its repaint.

25. AVIATION FUEL

Right: One of the heaviest single trainloads on the BR network was a daily working of 1,600 gross tonnes from Stanlow to Salfords oil depot, each train carrying 300,000 gallons of aviation kerosene for Gatwick airport until the service was replaced by a pipeline in 1984. Stanlow also despatched two or three trains of aviation fuel every month to the Rolls-Royce aero-engine factory at Sinfin, near Derby, while the twice-weekly trains to Shell's depot at Torksey, 10 miles north of Lincoln, regularly included tanks of aviation fuel alongside those loaded with motor spirit and diesel.

Until 1976 Shell and British Petroleum had operated a single rail tank wagon fleet controlled by Shell-Mex & BP Ltd, the joint distribution arm of the two companies, and years after this arrangement was abandoned it was still possible to find wagons painted in their original livery with the remains of both company logos. SUKO 60518, coded TTA, built by Metro-Cammell in 1966 and previously a TTF numbered SUKO 60123, was spotted at Ellesmere Port in December 1986. Shell's two-axle aviation-fuel tanks had been built with vacuum brakes and had TOPS numbers in the SUKO 601xx and 602xx series until renumbering into the SUKO 605xx, 606xx and 607xx series, albeit in a somewhat haphazard manner, after the fitting of air brakes in 1983.

Centre right: British Petroleum was the first oil company to take advantage of the relaxation in the livery requirement for Class A tank wagons and in 1990 adopted its house colours of bright green and yellow in lieu of the previously mandatory grey barrel and red solebars. At its Grangemouth refinery BP loaded trains for Prestwick Airport and the RAF bases at Leuchars and Lossiemouth, fuel for the latter destination being transferred to road tankers at Elgin. Following its takeover of Mobil's Coryton refinery in 1998 BP inherited a working to Langley for Heathrow Airport.

Repainted in 1992, BPO 37066 was one of several TTAs brought out of store to cope with the additional traffic from Coryton, although by June 2001 it was once again out of traffic at Stoke. Built by Pickering in 1965, it had been BPO 68279 before being fitted with air brakes and new suspension in 1981. Renumbered again in 2002 as BPO 60861, it was then allocated to Grangemouth. Aircraft jet engines run on Avtur (aviation turbine fuel), a high-octane kerosene with a low freezing-point suitable for high altitudes, and wagons in this traffic have either 1223 or 1863 UN hazard numbers.

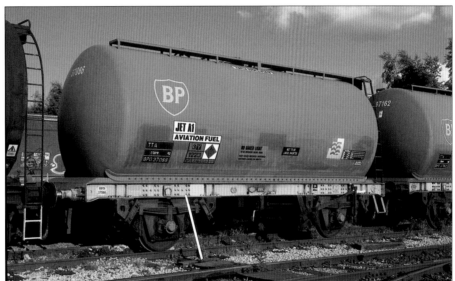

Above: The ELF terminal at Colnbrook was another destination for trainloads of Avtur, in this case for Heathrow and handled by a fleet of 18 bogie tanks, BRT 84193-200/314-21 and ELF 82315/6, these being used on workings from Unitank's West Thurrock terminal and from Gulf Oil's Waterston refinery at Milford Haven. Built by Standard Wagon in 1973 as a Class B tank for Total, BRT 84316 was recorded at Stoke in September 1998 while awaiting repair. All of this batch were fitted with Gloucester pedestal-suspension bogies as here, but at least one tank was noted subsequently running on Y25s.

Above: Prior to 1973 heavy oil had been the largest component of BR's petroleum business, and although the oil crisis resulted in a move towards cheaper sources of heating, many large concerns, such as British Steel and ICI, continued to receive block trains of fuel oil. Stanlow loaded two or three such trains a week for the ICI plants at Northwich and Runcorn and the Pilkington Glass factory in St Helens, and five or six bogie fuel-oil tanks were often attached to the daily mixed petroleum workings to Leeds and Jarrow.

The majority of Shell's bogie-tank fleet was built by Metro-Cammell in the 1960s to a design that lacked a continuous solebar, relying instead on the beam strength of the long barrel, which was secured by means of two short sections above each bogie, these 'solebars' then angling down and inwards to meet two steel members running from headstock to headstock along the underside of the tank. To keep the oil warm and assist discharge, Class B tanks in fuel-oil traffic were lagged and fitted with heating coils, one such being SUKO 83301, seen at Stanlow in July 1992.

Left: Shell also owned several batches of two-axle tanks, used for fuel oil, and as well as working in block trains these could be seen running in wagonload freights *en route* to the ICI works at Maxwelltown, near Dumfries, or Tees Store at Middlesbrough Dock Hill. SUKO 63831, built by Metro-Cammell in 1966, was recorded at Middlesbrough in September 1989.

Left: Lancashire Tar Distillers' 5,000,000gal-capacity oil depot at Weaste, three miles from the centre of Manchester, also received the occasional block train of fuel oil from Stanlow, but its main traffic comprised three trains weekly of DERV (for diesel-engined road vehicles) and kerosene from the Phillips refinery at Port Clarence, Teesside, and a weekly train of motor spirit from Mobil's Coryton refinery at Thames Haven. The depot at Weaste was reached by a single-track branch from the former Liverpool & Manchester Railway main line at Eccles, and all shunting was undertaken by Manchester Ship Canal Co locomotives — a lengthy and involved process, as the loop outside the depot could accommodate only seven bogie tanks. On 22 November 1990 the author arrived to find No D3, one of three MSC Hudswell Clarke 204hp 0-6-0DMs then based there, as the meat in a 'whale-belly' tank sandwich.

Right: The 'whale-belly' or oblate design, in which the barrel dipped below wheel height, had been developed in the United States, where it became very popular for liquid-petroleum-gas tanks. It never caught on in Britain, despite offering an extra 8 tons' capacity over more conventional designs, and Phillips Petroleum was the only company to lease a production batch, numbered PR 82730-47. Built by Procor in 1978 with an updated version of the Schlieren bogie, they were a common sight at Weaste depot, where PR 82737, loaded with 21,000 gallons of DERV, was photographed on 11 November 1990.

Left: In the 1980s the run-down of its refineries at Grain and Llandarcy left British Petroleum with surplus air-braked stock, much of which it leased to other oil companies, including 24 TTAs allocated to the motor-spirit flow from Coryton to Weaste, which were marked with a 'W' painted on the side. This train ran every Friday, arriving at Weaste shortly before lunch once the empties returning to Port Clarence had departed. On 22 March 1991 BPO 67768 was being unloaded at Weaste — a process that normally took a couple of hours. The oil depot was situated between the Ship Canal and Salford City Council Sewage Works, the resultant cocktail of odours making this a location to be avoided at the height of summer!

Right: Also situated on the north bank of the Manchester Ship Canal, nine miles west of Manchester, was the British Tar Products oil terminal at Glazebrook, the destination for train 6M08, which ran thrice-weekly conveying motor spirit from the ICI complex at Haverton Hill. This working gained notoriety on 20 December 1984, when the train derailed inside Summit Tunnel, near Todmorden, and in the ensuing conflagration, which lasted for 24 hours, 10 of its 13 tank wagons were destroyed. Among the replacements converted from redundant Class B tanks the following year was BRT 84129, noted passing Ashbury's on 18 July 1986.

While the former Class B tanks retained their Davies & Lloyd cast-steel bogies the conversion work entailed the removal of the steam coils, external cladding and insulation, the fitting of new manlids and vent valves, reconditioning of the outlet valves and replacement of gaskets and seals with items suitable for Class A products, and, at the request of ICI, buffer-override beams were added. The tanks were lettered for ICI Petrochemicals & Plastics Division and, unusually for this period, when most Class A tanks displayed the generic '1270' (a group number applicable to a range of petroleum products), these vehicles were clearly identified by their 1203 UN hazard number as being loaded with motor spirit. The wagons were also downrated to 91 tonnes glw and recoded TDA — an alteration that reflected the volumetric capacity of the vehicles, for as little as 65 tonnes of the light motor spirit was sufficient to fill the tank.

Below: In the months immediately following the accident ICI also leased a number of bogie tanks from BP as well as six spare TEAs from E. G. Steele. Between 1968 and 1970 CFPM had built 14 Class A bogie tanks for Total, and on TOPS these became STL 85701/2/22-30/41-3. Following their replacement at Lindsey in 1984 STL 85701/2/41-3 saw further use with Esso and Murco, in addition to ICI, but all were out of service by 1989. On 22 February 1985 STL 85743 was bringing up the rear of a working returning from Glazebrook, seen passing Ashburys.

Right: In 1988 ICI sold its petroleum-distribution business to Burmah, the tank wagons losing their ICI lettering, but the trains to Glazebrook continued, and on a wet day in June 1991 Class 47 No 47 212 was encountered shunting the morning arrival. As it had been raining for several days the author decided to avoid the lush vegetation at track level in favour of dry feet and grabbed this shot of PR 82694 (TOPS-coded TDB) as the train was propelled towards the terminal. Like BRT 84129 it had been converted in 1986 from a Class B wagon previously on hire to Total but, unlike the Metro-Cammell-built vehicle, had been constructed by Standard Wagon in 1970 with continuous solebars. However, the arrangement of end ladders and catwalks giving access to a central dipping hatch and two 18in-diameter manholes at 29ft 2in centres was fairly common to match the existing filling installations at the loading-points.

Left: Among the many batches of petroleum-tank wagons, some of the more unusual were the 14 Railease TEAs, RLS 82214-27, built at Heywood in 1980. Despite being lagged and coiled they appeared in Class A livery carrying kerosene and motor spirit from Lindsey to the Total distribution depot at Rectory Junction, near Nottingham RLS 82226 is seen passing through Nottingham station in March 1988.

Below: In 1989 the 14 Railease TEAs were repainted and transferred to fuel-oil traffic, becoming regular visitors to Glazebrook. RLS 82217 waits to return to Lindsey on 31 August 1993.

27. BITUMEN AND PETROLEUM COKE

Left: Bitumen, the residual fraction from the distillation of crude oil, is used in road construction, and, as it is not suitable for movement via pipeline, several rail flows ran to depots throughout the country. From its refineries at Ardrossan, Shellhaven and Stanlow Shell supplied more than 15 terminals, including Bardon Hill, Cranmore, Culloden Moor, Elswick, Exeter, Milnthorpe, Norwich, Skipton and West Drayton, until the traffic was lost to road in 1990. BP operated services from Llandarcy to Cardiff, Four Ashes, Grain and Kilnhurst, but with the closure of the bitumen plant in 1999 Llandarcy itself became the destination for a new working from Coryton. Both Shell and BP owned large fleets of 30-tonne-capacity, 46-tonne-glw two-axle bitumen tanks built in the 1960s by Metro-Cammell and Powell Duffryn, including BPO 61588 seen at Railcar Services, Stoke, in May 1986.

Centre left: In the early 1980s a number of Class B tanks were also converted into bitumen tanks for Shell and renumbered in the SUKO 613xx series. SUKO 61340, previously SUKO 65841, was photographed at Ellesmere Port in April 1985.

Below left: Certain grades of bitumen require a temperature of over 500°F before they flow freely, so many bitumen tanks are fitted with flame tubes in the end to enable the contents to be heated by means of portable burners, while some also have prominent 'chimneys' on top of the barrel.

In addition to its 46-tonners Shell also owned a small batch of 51-tonne-glw bitumen tanks and this type was also operated by Mobil and Lancashire Tar Distillers (LTD). The four LTD TUAs ran between the refinery at Lindsey near Immingham and the Lanfina terminal at Preston Docks, a facility owned jointly by Petrofina and LTD. Built by Standard Wagon in 1981, LTD 74500-3 were fitted with Gloucester pedestal suspension but unusually had the top filler located off-centre. However, like other bitumen TUAs they carried 35 tonnes of the sticky stuff. Most of the time the company logo was hidden beneath a layer of spilled bitumen, but a relatively clean LTD 74502 was found at Preston in February 1987.

Left and centre left: Some of the less-viscous grades of bitumen were carried in lagged and coiled Class B tanks such as BRT 57852, one of a batch of eight TTAs built at Heywood in 1970, and PR 70070, a TUA built by Standard Wagon in 1974. Both had originally been leased to Esso for fuel-oil traffic, but by 1993 they were working for Lanfina, being recorded in the exchange sidings at Preston Docks in August 1994.

Right: At most refineries the heavier components of crude oil are processed into fuel oil. However, Conoco opted to utilise a thermal cracking, coking and calcining plant at its Humber refinery, near Immingham, to convert these heavier oils into more valuable petroleum coke and lighter products. Several grades of petroleum coke were produced, the finest being used as a raw material in the manufacture of graphite electrodes. Built at BREL Doncaster in 1970 to coincide with the commissioning of the coking plant by Conoco, BRT 12100-16 constituted a unique batch of air-braked 33-tonne capacity, 46-tonne-glw covered hoppers coded PAB. Leased to Anglesey Aluminium, they worked as a weekly block train from Humber to the aluminium smelter at Holyhead until the traffic finished in 2001. BRT 12116 is seen in the refinery sidings at Immingham on 2 July 1996.

28. SHELL CHEMICALS

Left: In addition to its petroleum business Shell manufactured petrochemicals at two plants in Cheshire. At Partington the former Petrochemicals Ltd works produced thermoplastics such as polyethylene and polypropylene, while at Stanlow, alongside the refinery, Shell produced aromatics (such as benzene and toluene), detergents, plasticisers and solvents. The two plants were linked by pipeline, which limited rail traffic, but in the 1970s Shell Chemicals leased 15 BRTE Class A tanks to carry Linevol 79 (a highly linear alcohol, used to make plasticisers) from Stanlow to the BP Chemicals complex at Grangemouth. BRT 57822-8/32/3/5-40 were part of a batch of 19 wagons, built by Pickering in 1967, that had worked originally in block train formations on behalf of Murco from Grays to Bedworth, but with Shell these 45-ton tanks ran in wagonload freights. They also worked from Stanlow to the Royal Ordnance factories at Bishopton (with acetone) and Highbridge (toluene), and although most were withdrawn from traffic in 1983 BRT 57838/40, modified with parabolic springs so that they could run via Speedlink, continued to supply Highbridge until 1987. BRT 57837 was photographed in store at Railcar Services' Storrs Hill Works, Horbury, in August 1986.

Above: In 1985 Railcar Services in Stoke modified fifteen 45-ton Tiger Rail caustic-soda tanks from the series TRL 51586-648 to carry solvents on behalf of Shell Chemicals. The wagons' original running gear was replaced with FAT26 suspension with parabolic springs, while the barrels were replaced with those from withdrawn glycol and Class A ferry tanks used previously to carry acetaldehyde or hexylene glycol. Renumbered TRL 51954-68 and coded TTA, the modified wagons began to enter traffic in September 1985, allocated to pool 0625 for carrying acetone (a solvent used in the production of certain explosives) from Stanlow to Bishopton. By the following summer seven of the batch, TRL 51954/5/8/9/61-3, were in this pool, together with the two Tiger ferry tanks allocated to diagram E.343 (to be covered in a forthcoming volume). However, this seems to have been sufficient to meet the demand, as the others remained in store at Stoke. In 1987 Shell ceased to supply Bishopton, and most of these tanks were transferred to BP Chemicals at Hull, but TRL 51958/61-3 were retained at Stanlow to serve Roche at Dalry and Glaxo at Ulverston with acetone.

Having been in traffic for less than six months, TRL 51955 found itself back at Stoke in March 1986 with minor damage to the tank cladding, probably received at the loading racks at Stanlow. This wagon was constructed using the underframe from TRL 51624 and the barrel from acetaldehyde tank 23 70 7190 347.

Right: In 1975 Shell Chemicals leased from Procor 12 new 87-tonne-glw bogie tanks, numbered PR 78500-11, to carry propylene feedstock from the BP Chemicals plant at Baglan Bay, near Briton Ferry, to its works at Partington, and for this traffic Procor built three more tanks, PR 78400-2, in 1976. All were coded TCB and carried 51 tonnes, running on Y25C bogies. As described on page 95, five of Procor's redundant LPG tanks (PR 78533/5/8/40/1) were also allocated to this working in 1984, which saw a block train of between 10 and 14 tanks running twice a week to Partington, but the run-down of Baglan Bay meant that the service ended in 1993. Having lost its through vacuum pipe, TCA PR 78511 was noted at Northwich on 21 February 1988. The train had been stabled in Northwich Down Sidings, a points failure at Skelton Junction preventing access to the Partington branch.

Above: TRL 51961-3 were fitted with the larger-diameter barrels recovered from the three hexylene-glycol tanks allocated to ferry diagram E.311.

TRL 51961, which was built with the underframe from TRL 51628 and the tank from 21 70 0780 419, was recorded at Ellesmere Port in September 1991.

Left: Carbon dioxide (CO_2) is a by-product of the distillation of alcohol and of the manufacture of ammonia. In 1962 the Distillers Company leased from STS eight vacuum-braked 45-ton two-axle tank wagons, built by Motherwell Bridge & Engineering with double-link suspension, to carry liquid CO_2 from its distillery at Haymarket to Ardwick West Goods in Manchester, the CO_2 being destined for use by breweries and soft-drinks manufacturers throughout the North West of England. Subsequent years saw the traffic grow to encompass a number of other loading-points in Scotland, including Cameron Bridge, Cambus, Gartcosh and Mossend, and there was also considerable tonnage forwarded from the ICI fertiliser plants at Haverton Hill and Severn Beach. In addition to Ardwick regular destinations included Acton and Bow Goods in London and Coleshill in the West Midlands, while there were occasional workings to Barry, Bristol and Ipswich.

To handle the extra traffic an additional 61 CO_2 tanks were built between 1963 and 1978 (see table) with detailed differences between the batches. All had a heavily insulated barrel with loading and discharge valves located in a chest situated above the solebar behind a protective cover, while those forming the first batch from Fauvet Girel were ferry-fitted, although in fact they saw little if any use on the Continent. By 1977 all had been converted to air brakes and recoded TTA, while the Scottish-built vehicles had been fitted with Gloucester pedestal suspension, to conform with the rest of the fleet.

STS 53202, one of the original batch built in 1962, waits to be unloaded at Ardwick in January 1987. In common with all the CO_2 tanks built prior to 1974 the valve chest has a roller cover, but the large 'Distillers CO_2' lettering was to be found on only about a third of the fleet at this date.

Above: Following the closure in 1990 of Ardwick Goods, which had received up to a dozen tanks of CO_2 per week, some traffic was transferred to Newton-le-Willows, and STS 53240 was found being unloaded inside the old car compound on 6 September 1991. Its grubby condition, which was not untypical of these vehicles, contrasts with the recently repainted road tanker. Compared with the road tank's 15-tonne capacity the TTAs had a nominal payload of approximately 28 tonnes, although it was normal practice to limit them to 25 tonnes to allow for any increase in pressure during transit.

CO₂ tank wagons	
TOPS Nos	*Builder and date*
STS 53200-7	Motherwell Bridge & Engineering 1962
STS 53208-14	Motherwell Bridge & Engineering 1963/4
STS 53215-8	Motherwell Bridge & Engineering 1965/6
STS 53219-35	Fauvet Girel 1970
STS 53236-49	Fauvet Girel 1971
STS 53265-76	Fauvet Girel 1974
STS 53277-83	Fauvet Girel 1978

Right: Back at Ardwick in January 1987 STS 53274 is an example of the last two batches from Fauvet Girel, fitted with cupboard doors protecting the valve chest. Like the rest of the fleet it is painted in the livery mandatory for liquid gas tanks, for although CO_2 might have been less dangerous than many of the other chemicals transported by rail a major leakage could pose an inhalation hazard, particularly to yard ground staff.

Left: After the demise of Speedlink, block trains of CO_2 ran from Cameron Bridge and Haverton Hill to Coleshill and a new Distillers terminal at Willesden, and around the same time the wagons began to be repainted as they passed through works. STS 53241 shows off the new look at Stoke in July 1993

Left: There was no urgency in repainting the fleet, and less than half had been completed when the traffic ceased in March 1998. Later that year, when the wagons were cut up at Stoke, the author took this photograph of STS 53227, one of the ferry-fitted batch, to illustrate the thickness of the insulation on these tanks.

30. LPG TANKS

Left: British Petroleum, Esso, Mobil and Shell all owned or leased LPG (liquefied petroleum gas) tanks, the majority being either 35- or 40-ton-glw two-axle wagons, with capacities ranging from 16 to 21 tons, built between 1963 and 1967. Because butane and propane were carried as liquids under pressure the wagons required specially strengthened tank barrels, hence their relatively high tare weight.

In 1963 Esso purchased 40 vacuum-braked 35-ton tanks — 20 from Charles Roberts and 20 from Powell Duffryn — for a long-distance workings from its Herbrandston refinery at Milford Haven to the Scottish Gas Board's Lurgi gas plant at Thornton Junction, in Fife. The Lurgi process converted coal into almost pure methane, which had then to be 'sweetened' with LPG before it could be used by domestic customers. However, the plant at Thornton closed in 1969, and, as the country switched to North Sea gas, workings to other Gas Board sidings also ceased, and the Esso TSVs, ESSO 43101-40, were withdrawn from service during the 1970s. Originally they were fitted with large enamel plates bearing the Esso badge and had been painted white with two red vertical bands around the tank. However, this livery was replaced by the more familiar white with horizontal yellow/orange stripe in 1968. Following withdrawal from main-line use ESSO 43103 survived at Longport as a check-weight vehicle for the local LPG terminal and was recorded at the nearby Pinnox Branch Sidings in March 1991.

Centre left and left: Opened in 1969, the Esso LPG terminal at Longport received a daily block train from either Fawley or Herbrandston. ESSO 56377, built by Charles Roberts in 1965, was one of 65 Esso TTVs (ESSO 56341-405) to be fitted with air brakes in 1988, while ESSO 78036 came from a batch of 12 86-tonne-glw, 50-tonne-capacity TCBs (ESSO 78028-39), built at Horbury in 1970. Both were photographed at Longport in 1991.

Above: Esso also owned 27 92-tonne-glw TDAs (ESSO 78001-27) built by Pickering and Charles Roberts between 1968 and 1970, as well as a batch of eight more TCAs (ESSO 78041-48) constructed at Horbury in 1978, for in addition to the Longport traffic there were weekly trains of LPG to the aluminium smelter at Holyhead, the nickel works at Clydach-on-Tawe and the BOC distribution depot at Polmadie. Indeed, such was the traffic that Esso also leased a batch of 15 Procor TCAs built by Pickering in 1974. They were to a chassisless design whereby the tank barrel carried all the forces, the short stub-frames being simply a means of transferring the weight of the load to the Schlieren bogies. When the LPG traffic to Holyhead ended in 1984 many were stored at Stoke, including PR 78545, seen on a frosty morning in December 1985. Subsequently five tanks from the batch found further use carrying propylene for Shell Chemicals, but PR 78545 was not amongst them, being withdrawn the following year.

Below: Railcar Services at Stoke was a good place to find LPG tanks, for the hazardous nature of their load meant that they required more frequent maintenance than did other petroleum-tank wagons. A separate purging and testing area for LPG tanks was sited a short distance from the main works buildings, and SUKO 59612, built by Powell Duffryn in 1967, was one of four TTAs receiving attention on 14 June 1985. As the major hazard from LPG is its flammability the solebar-mounted warning plates are required to be painted red with white lettering. Other than relief valves these tanks had no top fittings, the loading, unloading and vapour-return valves being located in a recess in the side of the barrel, behind a lockable sliding panel.

Left: LPG traffic from Shell's Stanlow refinery was forwarded in wagonload freights to terminals in Elgin and Plymouth, while block trains ran to the British Aluminium smelter at Invergordon and the lime kilns at Hardendale. In addition to its two-axle fleet Shell owned 15 90-ton bogie LPG tanks built at Horbury between 1975 and 1980. Fitted with Gloucester pedestal-suspension bogies they also had end ladders, unique to this batch of LPG tanks. After LPG traffic from Stanlow ended in 1990, SUKO 89500-14 were stored at Connah's Quay, where SUKO 89508 was still awaiting disposal in September 1992.

Right and below right: In 1981, to instruct staff in the operation and maintenance of LPG tanks, an old Class B tank, SUKO 64214, was converted into a mobile training car. Internally the tank was fitted with the complex pipework of an LPG wagon, access for instruction being provided via a door in one end. Externally it lost its top filler, catwalk and end ladders but gained a side hatch. Air-piped and fitted with parabolic springs, it was renumbered SUKO 50000 and coded PXW. Based at Stanlow, it seems to have been a great favourite at rolling-stock exhibitions as well as doing the rounds of the wagon works. These two views, illustrating both ends of the vehicle, were recorded at Stoke in August 1988 and Aylesbury in May 1989.